# A Black Woman's
# Civil War Memoirs

*Susie King Taylor.*

# Susie King Taylor

*Reminiscences of My Life in Camp
with the 33rd U.S. Colored Troops,
Late 1st South Carolina Volunteers*

# A Black Woman's
# Civil War Memoirs

Edited with commentary by
Patricia W. Romero

and with a new introduction by
Willie Lee Rose

Markus Wiener
Publishers
PRINCETON

Eighth printing, 2009.

*Reminiscences of My Life in Camp with the 33rd U.S. Colored Troops, Late 1st South Carolina Volunteers* was first published by the author, Susie King Taylor, in 1902 in Boston.

For information write to:
Markus Wiener Publishers
231 Nassau Street, Princeton, NJ 08542
www.markuswiener.com

**Library of Congress Cataloging-in-Publication Data**
Taylor, Susie King, b. 1848.
    [Reminiscences of my life in camp]
    A black woman's Civil War memoirs : reminiscences of my life in camp
with the 33rd U.S. Colored Troops, late 1st South Carolina Volunteers /
Susie King Taylor ; edited by Patricia W. Romero; with a new introduction
by Willie Lee Rose.—1st M. Wiener Pub. ed.
    Reprint. Originally published: Reminiscences of my life in camp
with the 33d United States Colored Troops, late 1st S.C. Volunteers.
Boston : S.K. Taylor, 1902. With new introd.
    Bibliography: p.
    ISBN 978-0-910129-85-5 (pbk.)
    1. Taylor, Susie King, b. 1848.  2. United States. Army. South Carolina
Volunteers, First—Biography.  3. United States—History—Civil War, 1861-
1865—Personal narratives.  4. United States—History—Civil War, 1861-
1865—Regimental histories.  5. United States—History—Civil War, 1861-
1865—Afro-Americans.  6. United States—History—Civil War, 1861-
1865—Participation, Afro-American. 7. Afro-Americans— South Carolina
—Biography.  8. South Carolina— Biography.  I. Romero, Patricia W.  II.
Title.  III. Title: Reminiscences of my life in camp with the 33rd U.S.
Colored Troops, late 1st South Carolina Volunteers. E492.94 33rd.
T3 1988 973.7'415—dc19
[B] 87-33407                                          CIP

Photos from the collection of Patricia W. Romero.
Reprinted in *Negro Americans in the Civil War,*
edited by Charles H. Wesley and Patricia W. Romero (1967).

Printed in the United States of America on acid-free paper.

# INTRODUCTION
## BY
# WILLIE LEE ROSE
Johns Hopkins University

THERE IS nothing even vaguely resembling Susie King Taylor's small volume of random recollections in the entire literature of the Civil War, or in that of any other American conflict insofar as I am aware. These are the memoirs of a black woman who was born a slave, who had the good fortune to gain her freedom early in the war, with the education and ability to observe and the will to recall in later years, the significance of the events in which she was a vigorous participant.

Mrs. Taylor began her connection with the Union Army one morning in early April of 1862, when, she tells us, she was brought aboard a Federal gunboat from St. Catherine's, a small island not far south of Savannah. Young Susie was only fourteen years old at the time, and was in the company of an uncle who had seized upon the opportunity afforded by the Federal attack on Fort Pulaski, the guardian fortress of Savannah harbor, to place his own family and young Susie outside the reach of the Confederate authorities.

What Mrs. Taylor does not remember to tell us about the event, is that the action her family had taken was in direct response to the most exciting lure conceivable to slaves: freedom. Much of the rare value of Mrs. Taylor's book is owing to her having gained her freedom so early in the war, and having been in consequence, in a position to observe some of the most interesting "firsts" of the Civil War.

On April 12, 1862, Major-General David Hunter, in command of the Department of the South, made a successful assault on Fort Pulaski, and immediately announced that all slaves in the immediate vicinity of the Fort would be regarded as free men. This was the second such step taken during the war, but the first that President Lincoln did not countermand. Earlier in the war, which was by now a year old, General John G. Frémont had attempted to get the same emancipating policy adopted in Missouri. President Lincoln had then rebuked Frémont by countermanding his order. This time he did not renounce Hunter's action, and men observed that Edwin Stanton, Lincoln's new Secretary of War, was a man of strong antislavery inclinations, just as Frémont and Hunter were.

Slaves had presented problems of status once they escaped to the Federal lines, but all these had been resolved before Hunter's attack on Fort Pulaski by the fairly expedient formula of categorizing such escapees as "contraband of war" and refusing to return them to their masters. Although this policy had had a tremendous advantage as compared with the policy of returning slaves followed by some officers in the first months of the conflict, it was still a very insecure hold on freedom from the runaway's point of view. Therefore General Hunter's new policy was welcomed by anti-slavery men and women everywhere, and particularly by slaves, as an indication of still better things to come. The impact of this news resulted immediately in an increasing number of fugitives within the Federal lines in the whole coastal area between Charleston and Savannah. Therefore one supposes that it was not by chance that Susie's family gathered so near the guns of Fort Pulaski.

Very shortly this family of escapees found itself involved deeply in another Civil War "first." In no time Susie's uncle and many of her fellow escapees from Georgia were enlisted in a newly-forming regiment of black soldiers being organized under the charge of General Hunter at the headquarters of his army on Port Royal Island, north of Savannah on the South Carolina coast. The South Carolina Sea Islands had been occupied in the fall of 1861 as a means of providing a haven in stormy weather for the Federal blockading squadrons that patrolled the coastline and as a good location for the training of raw recruits from the North during the first winter of the war. Although the choice of this particularly vulnerable district was made with no particular reference to the demography of the region, the fact that the population was composed almost entirely of slaves was to prove to be of enormous significance in the course of the war. Only 17 percent of the population of the islands stretched along the coast south of Charleston was white; the rest were slaves who had lived in the greatest possible isolation from the outside world. When their masters fled in haste from the invading forces of the Union Army, the slaves remained on the plantations, relieved no doubt to be rid of one set of masters, but uneasy about what the future held in store.

One of the largest cotton crops in recent memory was also largely abandoned by the retreating Confederates, and the juxtaposition of the slaves and the cotton formed the rationale for a highly interesting and experimental effort to demonstrate that the blacks would work at securing this cotton to the United States Treasury Department for wages, and without compulsion. Although Susie King Taylor does not tell us about this recent development in the island country where she came to live and work during the war, it is a very important fact in the background of her story. The region had become a proving ground for freedom, and had attracted many Northern men and women of antislavery conviction, who came to supervise the planting of cotton on a free labor basis, to teach the ex-slaves to read and write, and to play a semi-paternal role in the period of transition from slavery to freedom that the people of the islands were experiencing. It was therefore not surprising that the first black soldiers to fight in the Union armies were enlisted in this theater of the war. Although Hunter's little band of recruits was not immediately recognized by the War Department, and was partially disbanded in the summer of the same spring it was organized, it was not entirely dissolved before official recognition came. The unit was reconstituted in August under the ironic denomination of the First South Carolina Volunteers, led by an antislavery officer of national reputation, Colonel Thomas Wentworth Higginson. This was the regiment that several of the men of Susie's family had joined, and the regiment in which she became a most extraordinary laundress.

Because she had learned to read and write while still a slave girl in Savannah, Susie found herself doing as much teaching as washing and ironing. As a part of the classic tableau of the black soldier bending over his book in the light of the campfire, Susie found her services in great demand. According to Colonel Higginson, whose *Army Life in a Black Regiment* has

become a minor classic of Civil War literature,
the soldiers' "love of the spelling-book" was
"perfectly inexhaustible," and those who held
the key to it were constantly pressed into service.

Once the troops engaged in combat, Susie
found further usefulness in nursing the
wounds of soldiers, men cut down in the
small-scale but sanguinary encounters that
marked the semi-guerilla fighting along the
marshy coastline of South Carolina, Georgia,
and Florida. The most famous of these engagements was the assault on Battery Wagner,
which controlled Charleston Harbor. This
struggle, which took place on July 18th of 1863,
was one of several engagements in that year
that demonstrated to skeptical Northern opinion, that the black man was a formidable soldier, and an ally of great potential. The soldiers
who distinguished, indeed, immolated themselves, were men of the 54th Massachusetts
Volunteers, free blacks from the North, but
because they were stationed in the same region
as Susie King Taylor's regiment, she formed a
part of their nursing corps, and these men
became "our boys" to her, as the men of the
First South Carolina already were.

These were exciting times for a young girl
not out of her teens, and Susie King Taylor's
recollections of them are invaluable for those
who wish to understand the Civil War from
the black woman's point of view. One wishes,

however, that Susie had written as much about herself as she wrote about "our boys." What no doubt seemed to her of little consequence would have been treasured today in light of the feminist movement. That in 1862 she married Edward King, a sergeant in Colonel Higginson's regiment, is given only passing mention, and that she was only seventeen at the end of the war must be calculated through simple arithmetic. The trials of the months at the end of the war, when the Kings came back to Savannah and Susie opened a private school for black children, are indicated in the sketchiest of outlines. What were the thoughts of a young mother-to-be upon the sudden and accidental death of her husband, the reader must only guess. Mrs. King's second marriage, contracted when she was thirty-one, to Russell L. Taylor, is recorded with equal brevity.

Young Susie was not thoroughly aware of the unique character of the sector of the war in which she participated, or of the white people with whom her lot was cast. The inability to set her war experiences into a wider perspective results through no fault of Susie's, but it deprives the reader of a certain detachment that must be supplied on one's own. It also explains in part the shock and disillusionment Mrs. Taylor experienced in the 1890s—post-Reconstruction—when she was obliged to observe at last the shallowness of the national commitment to equality, a commitment she had trusted completely at the time it was being made.

On the other hand, what Susie King Taylor described, she described with economy and feeling, in a forthright and unadorned chronicle of events. "It was a glorious day for us all," she recalls of the celebration held on January 1, 1863, of Lincoln's Emancipation Proclamation. She found herself among the only gathering of blacks anywhere in the country where the Proclamation could have had an effective emancipatory function, for other occupied areas of the South were specifically excluded from the terms of the Proclamation. It was, nevertheless, an important turning point in the war, the official advent of a policy that had been subtly inaugurated in August of 1862, when the War Department gave its blessing to the recruitment of black soldiers.

Among the most interesting sections of Mrs. King's book are those dealing with the reactions of her grown-up relatives to the prospect of freedom opened up by the war, and the nervousness of the white population about that reaction. The usual prayer-meetings could no longer be tolerated when "freedom" of the heavenly future might conceivably be interpreted by the slaves as an earthly possibility. "Oh, how these people prayed for freedom." It is remarkable how much insight the reader may gain on slavery from the few pages Mrs. Taylor gave to the theme at the beginning of her book.

The striking figure of her grandmother eclipses others who emerge less distinctly from the shadows of that old life. Susie's grandmother got enough money through steady application to her chicken and egg barter with the plantation slaves to invest in the Freedmen's Bank after the war, money which she lost, of course, when the bank failed. But she had the detachment not to hate the Yankees for the result. "I will leave it all in God's hand. If the Yankees did take all our money, they freed my race; God will take care of us." The shrewd head for business appears from Susie's account to have descended through the maternal line, and in this respect her story reinforces the view of slavery as matri-focal in its family organization. Susie's mother, by her account, managed to secure seven hundred acres of land in the post-bellum period, an astonishing amount of real estate for anyone, black or white, to have accumulated in that period.

Susie King Taylor went North after the war, and led a full life of service. She never forgot "our boys," and from her home in Boston found the time and energy for an active part in the work of the Women's Relief Corps. She scrutinized national policy for racial implications, and charged the United States with bringing a kind of racism to Cuba that was unknown there before. She never ceased to wave the bloody shirt, for she could not forget the horrors of the war, and she reminds the

United Daughters of the Confederacy of their blindness in regard to the barbarities committed daily upon Southern blacks.

The close of Mrs. King's book makes plain her indignation over the betrayal of the black men who had fought for the Union. She does not probe deeply the responsibility national leaders must bear for the betrayal before the bar of history, even though one reads between the lines that she is aware of it. Nor does Mrs. King seem fully aware of the not-so-subtle economic disadvantages her race endured in the North in this "nadir" of race relations. And yet, Mrs. King struggles for understanding, and a hopeful view of the future. Her passionate and disillusioned closing pages are saved from despair by her faith that ultimately justice will prevail.

There seems no reason to question the authenticity of Mrs. King's work. We may believe Colonel Higginson's immodest and somewhat presumptuous remark that he only changed the spelling of proper names, with the implied suggestion that the work might have been more stylish had he done more. Although the tempo and urgency Mrs. Taylor's account accelerates sharply when she moves from what she remembered of the war to what she was experiencing at the time of writing, the style of the work remains basically the same, and it remains what Colonel Higginson said it was, "the plain record of simple lives led in stormy periods." The simplicity of Mrs. King's life, however, is simple only as the world in its simplicity judges these matters.

Willie Lee Rose
Baltimore, Maryland
December, 1987

# REMINISCENCES OF
# MY LIFE IN CAMP

**WITH THE 33D UNITED STATES
COLORED TROOPS LATE 1ST
S. C. VOLUNTEERS**

BY

## SUSIE KING TAYLOR

*WITH ILLUSTRATIONS*

**BOSTON**
**PUBLISHED BY THE AUTHOR**
1902

*Original Title Page*

# CONTENTS

# INTRODUCTION

ACTUAL military life is rarely described by a woman, and this is especially true of a woman whose place was in the ranks, as the wife of a soldier and herself a regimental laundress. No such description has ever been given, I am sure, by one thus connected with a colored regiment; so that the nearly 200,000 black soldiers (178,975) of our Civil War have never before been delineated from the woman's point of view. All this gives peculiar interest to this little volume, relating wholly to the career of the very earliest of these regiments,—the one described by myself, from a wholly different point of view, in my volume "Army Life in a Black Regiment," long since translated into French by the Comtesse de Gasparin under the title "Vie Militaire dans un Régiment Noir."

The writer of the present book was very exceptional among the colored laundresses, in that she could read and write and had taught children to do the same; and her whole life and career were most estimable, both during the war and in the later period during which she has lived in Boston and has made many friends. I may add that I did not see the book until the sheets were in print, and have left it wholly untouched, except as to a few errors in proper names. I commend the narrative to those who love the plain record of simple lives, led in stormy periods.


THOMAS WENTWORTH HIGGINSON,
Former Colonel 1st S. C. Volunteers
(afterwards 33d U. S. Colored Infantry).

Cambridge, Mass.,
November 3, 1902

# REMINISCENCES

## I
## A BRIEF SKETCH OF MY ANCESTORS[1]

My great-great-grandmother was 120 years old when she died. She had seven children, and five of her boys were in the Revolutionary War. She was from Virginia, and was half Indian. She was so old she had to be held in the sun to help restore or prolong her vitality.

My great-grandmother, one of her daughters, named Susanna, was married to Peter Simons,[2] and was one hundred years old when she died, from a stroke of paralysis in Savannah. She was the mother of twenty-four children, twenty-three being girls. She was one of the noted midwives of her day. In 1820 my grandmother was born, and named after her grandmother, Dolly, and in 1833 she married Fortune Lambert Reed. Two children blessed their union, James and Hagar Ann. James died at the age of twelve years.

My mother was born in 1834. She married

Raymond Baker in 1847. Nine children were born to them, three dying in infancy. I was the first born. I was born on the Grest Farm (which was on an island known as Isle of Wight),[3] Liberty County, about thirty-five miles from Savannah, Ga., on August 6, 1848, my mother being waitress for the Grest family. I have often been told by mother of the care Mrs. Grest took of me. She was very fond of me, and I remember when my brother and I were small children, and Mr. Grest would go away on business, Mrs. Grest would place us at the foot of her bed to sleep and keep her company. Sometimes he would return home earlier than he had expected to; then she would put us on the floor.

When I was about seven years old, Mr. Grest allowed[4] my grandmother to take my brother and me to live with her in Savannah. There were no railroad connections in those days between this place and Savannah; all travel was by stagecoaches. I remember, as if it were yesterday, the coach which ran in from Savannah, with its driver, whose beard nearly reached his knees. His name was Shakespeare, and often I would go to the stable where he kept his horses, on Barnard Street in front of the old Arsenal, just to look at his wonderful beard.

My grandmother went every three months to see my mother. She would hire a wagon to carry bacon, tobacco, flour, molasses, and sugar. These she would trade with people in the neighboring places, for eggs, chickens, or cash, if they had it. These, in turn, she carried back to the city market, where she had a customer who sold them for her. The profit from these, together with laundry work and care of some bachelors' rooms, made a good living for her.

The hardest blow to her was the failure of the Freedmen's Savings Bank in Savannah,[5] for in that bank she had placed her savings, about three thousand dollars, the result of her hard labor and self-denial before the war, and which, by dint of shrewdness and care, she kept together all through the war. She felt it more keenly, coming as it did in her old age, when her life was too far spent to begin anew; but she took a practical view of the matter, for she said, "I will leave it all in God's hand. If the Yankees did take all our money, they freed my race; God will take care of us."

In 1888 she wrote me here (Boston), asking me to visit her, as she was getting very feeble and wanted to see me once before she passed away. I made up my mind to leave at once, but about the time I planned to go, in March, a fearful blizzard swept our country, and travel was at a standstill for nearly two weeks; but March 15 I left on the first through steamer from New York, en route for the South, where I again saw my grandmother, and we felt thankful that we were spared to meet each other once more. This was the last time I saw her, for in May, 1889, she died.

Notes on chapter *I*.

[1] The ancestors mentioned here are all matri-lineal, i.e., from the mother's side.

[2] The usual slave marriage consisted of finding a partner among the slaves on the same plantation and having the master bless the union. Slave marriages were not considered legal, and were dissolved and sometimes ignored fairly easily. Besides, husbands, wives, and children were often separated by sale. Despite these handicaps, many slaves managed to maintain some semblance of marriage, and enjoyed with their children the small degree of family life which slavery allowed them.

[3] This is one of the sea islands off the coast of South Carolina and Georgia, location of some of the largest and richest plantations in the antebellum South. Only the warm, wet sea islands could support the growth of the high quality, long staple cotton—the most lucrative variety to grow before the invention of the cotton gin. Generally, the slaves there were among the most disadvantaged, and their isolation from the mainland kept them from contacts which could make their transition to freedom easier.

[4] The master, not the parent, had control over the destinies of slave children. Dolly Reed, Susie's grandmother, appears to have been freed by Mr. Grest, who remained her guardian. Every freedman was required to have a white guardian. Mr. Grest's action in allowing the children to go to Savannah may have been tantamount to freeing them. Freedom was admittedly better than slavery, but it was not necessarily a happy state. Most freedmen lived poorly in the back street ghettoes of towns, for city life offered more opportunities, slim as they were, than country life.

[5] The Freedmen's Bank failed in 1874. Chartered by Congress in 1865 to encourage thrift among the newly-freed slaves, branches had been established in major cities of the North and South. It came under the control of white financiers who were reckless with the funds. It was a time of corruption in big business and banking, when monetary laws were lax or nonexistent.

## II
## MY CHILDHOOD


I was born under the slave law in Georgia, in
1848, and was brought up by my grandmother
in Savannah. There were three of us with her,
my younger sister and brother. My brother and
I being the two eldest, we were sent to a friend
of my grandmother, Mrs. Woodhouse, a
widow, to learn to read and write.[1] She was a
free woman and lived on Bay Lane, between
Habersham and Price streets, about half a mile
from my house. We went every day about nine
o'clock, with our books wrapped in paper to
prevent the police or white persons from
seeing them. We went in, one at a time,
through the gate, into the yard to the L
kitchen, which was the schoolroom. She had
twenty-five or thirty children whom she
taught, assisted by her daughter, Mary Jane.
The neighbors would see us going in sometimes, but they supposed we were there learn-
ing trades, as it was the custom to give children

29

a trade of some kind. After school we left the same way we entered, one by one, when we would go to a square, about a block from the school, and wait for each other. We would gather laurel leaves and pop them on our hands, on our way home. I remained at her school for two years or more, when I was sent to a Mrs. Mary Beasley, where I continued until May, 1860, when she told my grand-mother she had taught me all she knew, and grandmother had better get some one else who could teach me more, so I stopped my studies for a while.

I had a white playmate about this time, named Katie O'Connor, who lived on the next corner of the street from my house, and who attended a convent. One day she told me, if I would promise not to tell her father, she would give me some lessons. On my promise not to do so, and getting her mother's consent, she gave me lessons about four months, every eve-ning. At the end of this time she was put into the convent permanently, and I have never seen her since.

A month after this, James Blouis, our land-lord's son, was attending the High School,[2] and was very fond of grandmother, so she asked him to give me a few lessons, which he did until the middle of 1861, when the Savan-nah Volunteer Guards, to which he and his brother belonged, were ordered to the front under General Barton. In the first battle of

Manassas,[3] his brother Eugene was killed, and James deserted over to the Union side, and at the close of the war went to Washington, D.C., where he has since resided.

I often wrote passes for my grandmother, for all colored persons, free or slaves, were compelled to have a pass; free colored people having a guardian in place of a master. These passes were good until 10 or 10.30 P.M. for one night or every night for one month. The pass read as follows:—

SAVANNAH, GA., MARCH 1ST, 1860.
Pass the bearer_____from 9 to 10.30. P.M.
Valentine Grest.

Every person had to have this pass, for at nine o'clock each night a bell was rung, and any colored persons found on the street after this hour were arrested by the watchman, and put in the guard-house until next morning, when their owners would pay their fines and release them. I knew a number of persons who went out at any time at night and were never arrested, as the watchman knew them so well he never stopped them, and seldom asked to see their passes, only stopping them long enough, sometimes, to say "Howdy," and then telling them to go along.

About this time I had been reading[4] so much about the "Yankees" I was very anxious to see them. The whites would tell their colored people not to go to the Yankees, for they would harness them to carts and make them pull the carts around, in place of horses. I asked grandmother, one day, if this was true. She replied, "Certainly not!" that the white people did not want slaves to go over to the Yankees, and told them these things to frighten them. "Don't you see those signs pasted about the streets? one reading, 'I am a rattlesnake, if you touch me I will strike!' Another reads, 'I am a wildcat! Beware,' etc. These are warnings to the North; so don't mind what the white people say." I wanted to see these wonderful "Yankees" so much, as I heard my parents say the Yankee was going to set all the slaves free. Oh, how those people prayed for freedom! I remember, one night, my grandmother went out into the suburbs of the city to a church meeting, and they were fervently singing this old hymn,—

> "Yes, we all shall be free,
> Yes, we all shall be free,
> Yes, we all shall be free,
> When the Lord shall appear,"—

when the police came in and arrested all who were there, saying they were planning freedom, and sang "the Lord,"[5] in place of "Yankee," to blind any one who might be listening. Grandmother never forgot that night, although she did not stay in the guard-house, as she sent to her guardian, who came at once for her; but this was the last meeting she ever attended out of the city proper.

On April 1, 1862, about the time the Union soldiers were firing on Fort Pulaski, I was sent out into the country to my mother.[6] I remember what a roar and din the guns made. They jarred the earth for miles. The fort was at last taken by them. Two days after the taking of Fort Pulaski, my uncle took his family of seven and myself to St. Catherine Island.[7] We landed under the protection of the Union fleet, and remained there two weeks, when about thirty of us were taken aboard the gunboat P_____, to be transferred to St. Simon's Island;[8] and at last, to my unbounded joy, I saw the "Yankee."

After we were all settled aboard and started on our journey, Captain Whitmore, commanding the boat, asked me where I was from. I told him Savannah, Ga. He asked if I could read; I said, "Yes!" "Can you write?" he next asked. "Yes, I can do that also," I replied, and as if he had some doubts of my answers he handed me a book and a pencil and told me to write my name and where I was from. I did this; when he wanted to know if I could sew. On hearing I could, he asked me to hem some napkins for him. He was surprised at my accomplishments (for they were such in those days), for he said he did not know there were any negroes in the South able to read or write. He said, "You seem to be so different from the other colored people who came from the same place you

did." "No!" I replied, "the only difference is,
they were reared in the country and I in the
city, as was a man from Darien, Ga., named
Edward King." That seemed to satisfy him,
and we had no further conversation that day
on the subject.

In the afternoon the captain spied a boat in
the distance, and as it drew nearer he noticed it
had a white flag hoisted, but before it had
reached the Putumoka he ordered all passengers between decks, so we could not be
seen, for he thought they might be spies. The
boat finally drew alongside of our boat, and
had Mr. Edward Donegall on board, who
wanted his two servants, Nick and Judith. He
wanted these, as they were his own children.
Our captain told him he knew nothing of
them, which was true, for at the time they were
on St. Simon's, and not, as their father supposed, on our boat. After the boat left, we were
allowed to come up on deck again.

Notes on chapter *II.*

[1] Occasionally a slave child would be taught the rudiments of reading or writing by his master on the plantation, but the laws forbidding the education of blacks were strictly obeyed otherwise. Education for blacks was held to be dangerous, because of the quite reasonable fear that educated slaves would not tolerate submission. Slavery had no room for new ideas. The education of black children, therefore, had to be carried on surreptitiously. In Virginia and South Carolina free Negro children were whipped if they were found getting any schooling.

[2] Every southern state chartered public schools for whites, although these schools were neither numerous nor adequate. The upper classes instituted their own private academies (there were 3,000 throughout the South in 1850) or had private tutors. The poor whites, for the most part, viewed education as an impractical frill.

[3] At the first Battle of Manassas, the first real confrontation of troops in the Civil War, and a Confederate victory, there were 5,000 casualties, 2,000 of them Southerners.

[4] Newspapers reported the events leading up to the war, many of which had to do with antislavery activity in the North. The Yankee thus became identified as the friend of blacks and the enemy of the white Southerner.

[5] Slaves at Georgetown, South Carolina, were whipped for celebrating Lincoln's election by singing a hymn with the verse: "We'll soon be free Till de Lord shall call us home." The Southerners accused the slaves of meaning "the Yankees" when singing "the Lord."

[6] Susie Baker was now fourteen years old.

[7] This is one of the Georgia Sea Islands, south of Savannah. With the capture of Fort Pulaski on April 12, 1862, the Union occupied the Georgia coast and Sea Islands, adding that to the South Carolina coast and Sea Islands, secured during the Port Royal Expedition in November, 1861. Charleston was then the only major port along that coast still held by the Confederates. Many slaves fled plantations on the Union-occupied land, and gathered at the Union encampments on the islands. In the meantime, the Sea Islands were deserted by the white plantation owners, whose cotton crops were taken over by the U.S. Treasury Department, using the black laborers who were now declared "contraband of war," a status never made quite clear.

ᵏSt. Simon's Island is south of St. Catherine's Island, near the town of Darien, at the mouth of the Altamaha River. This is the area described by Frances Kemble in her *Journal of a Residence on a Georgia Plantation in 1838–1839.*

# III
# ON ST. SIMON'S ISLAND
# 1862

NEXT morning we arrived at St. Simon's, and
the captain told Commodore Goldsborough
about this affair, and his reply was, "Captain
Whitmore, you should not have allowed them
to return, you should have kept them." After I
had been on St. Simon's about three days,
Commodore Goldsborough heard of me, and
came to Gaston Bluff[1] to see me. I found him
very cordial. He said Captain Whitmore had
spoken to him of me, and that he was pleased
to hear of my being so capable, etc., and
wished me to take charge of a school for the
children on the island. I told him I would
gladly do so, if I could have some books. He
said I should have them, and in a week or two I
received two large boxes of books and testa-
ments from the North.[2] I had about forty children to teach, besides a number of adults who
came to me nights, all of them so eager to learn

to read, to read above anything else. Chaplain French,[3] of Boston, would come to the school, sometimes, and lecture to the pupils on Boston and the North.

About the first of June we were told that there was going to be a settlement of the war. Those who were on the Union side would remain free, and those in bondage were to work three days for their masters and three for themselves. It was a gloomy time for us all, and we were to be sent to Liberia. Chaplain French asked me would I rather go back to Savannah or go to Liberia.[4] I told him the latter place by all means. We did not know when this would be, but we were prepared in case this settlement should be reached. However, the Confederates would not agree to the arrangement, or else it was one of the many rumors flying about at the time, as we heard nothing further of the matter. There were a number of settlements on this island of St. Simon's, just like little villages, and we would go from one to the other on business, to call, or only for a walk.

One Sunday, two men, Adam Miller and Daniel Spaulding, were chased by some rebels as they were coming from Hope Place (which was between the Beach and Gaston Bluff), but the latter were unable to catch them. When they reached the Beach and told this, all the men on the place, about ninety, armed themselves, and next day (Monday), with Charles

O'Neal as their leader, skirmished the island for the "rebs." In a short while they discovered them in the woods, hidden behind a large log, among the thick underbrush. Charles O'Neal was the first to see them, and he was killed; also John Brown, and their bodies were never found.[5] Charles O'Neal was an uncle of Edward King,[6] who later was my husband and a sergeant in Co. E., U.S. I. Another man was shot, but not found for three days. On Tuesday, the second day, Captain Trowbridge[7] and some soldiers landed, and assisted the skirmishers. Word having been sent by the mailboat Uncas to Hilton Head,[8] later in the day Commodore Goldsborough, who was in command of the naval station, landed about three hundred marines, and joined the others to oust the rebels. On Wednesday, John Baker, the man shot on Monday, was found in a terrible condition by Henry Batchlott, who carried him to the Beach, where he was attended by the surgeon. He told us how, after being shot, he lay quiet for a day. On the second day he managed to reach some wild grapes growing near him. These he ate, to satisfy his hunger and intense thirst, then he crawled slowly, every movement causing agony, until he got to the side of the road. He lived only three months after they found him.

On the second day of the skirmish the troops captured a boat which they knew the Confederates had used to land in, and having this in their possession, the "rebs" could not return; so pickets were stationed all around the island. There was an old man, Henry Capers, who had been left on one of the places by his old master, Mr. Hazzard, as he was too old to carry away. These rebels went to his house in the night, and he hid them up in the loft.[9] On Tuesday all hands went to this man's house with a determination to burn it down, but Henry Batchlott pleaded with the men to spare it. The rebels were in hiding, still, waiting a chance to get off the island. They searched his house, but neglected to go up into the loft, and in so doing missed the rebels concealed there. Late in the night Henry Capers gave them his boat to escape in, and they got off all right. This old man was allowed by the men in charge of the island to cut grass for his horse, and to have a boat to carry this grass to his home, and so they were not detected, our men thinking it was Capers using the boat. After Commodore Goldsborough left the island, Commodore Judon sent the old man over to the mainland and would not allow him to remain on the island.

There were about six hundred men, women, and children on St. Simon's, the women and children being in the majority, and we were afraid to go very far from our own quarters in the daytime, and at night even to go out of the house for a long time; for there were not any soldiers on the island, only the marines who

were on the gunboats along the coast. The
rebels, knowing this, could steal by them
under cover of the night, and getting on the
island would capture any persons venturing
out alone and carry them to the mainland.[10]
Several of the men disappeared, and as they
were never heard from we came to the conclusion they had been carried off in this way.

The latter part of August, 1862, Captain C. T.
Trowbridge, with his brother John and Lieutenant Walker, came to St. Simon's Island from
Hilton Head, by order of General Hunter, to
get all the men possible to finish filling his
regiment which he had organized in March,
1862.[11] He had heard of the skirmish on this
island, and was very much pleased at the bravery shown by these men. He found me at
Gaston Bluff teaching my little school, and was
much interested in it. When I knew him better
I found him to be a thorough gentleman and a
staunch friend to my race.

Captain Trowbridge remained with us until
October, when the order was received to evacuate, and so we boarded the Ben-De-Ford, a
transport, for Beaufort, S.C. When we arrived
in Beaufort, Captain Trowbridge and the men
he had enlisted went to camp at Old Fort,
which they named "Camp Saxton." I was enrolled as laundress.

The first suits worn by the boys were red
coats and pants, which they disliked very
much, for, they said, "The rebels see us, miles

away."[12]

The first colored troops did not receive any pay for eighteen months, and the men had to depend wholly on what they received from the commissary, established by General Saxton. A great many of these men had large families, and as they had no money to give them, their wives were obliged to support themselves and children by washing for the officers of the gunboats and the soldiers, and making cakes and pies which they sold to the boys in camp. Finally, in 1863, the government decided to give them half pay, but the men would not accept this. They wanted "full pay" or nothing. They preferred rather to give their services to the state, which they did until 1864, when the government granted them full pay, with all the back pay due.[13]

I remember hearing Captain Heasley telling his company, one day, "Boys, stand up for your full pay! I am with you, and so are all the officers." This captain was from Pennsylvania, and was a very good man, all the men liked him. N. G. Parker, our first lieutenant, was from Massachusetts. H. A. Beach was from New York. He was very delicate, and had to resign in 1864 on account of ill health.

I had a number of relatives in this regiment,—several uncles, some cousins, and a husband in Company E, and a number of cousins in other companies. Major Strong, of this regiment, started home on a furlough, but

Capt. A. W. Heasley
Capt. Walker                    Capt. W. W. Sampson
Capt. Charles E. Parker

the vessel he was aboard was lost, and he never reached his home. He was one of the best officers we had. After his death, Captain C. T. Trowbridge was promoted major, August, 1863, and filled Major Strong's place until December, 1864, when he was promoted lieutenant-colonel, which he remained until he was mustered out, February 6, 1866.

In February, 1863, several cases of varioloid[14] broke out among the boys, which caused some anxiety in camp. Edward Davis, of Company E (the company I was with), had it very badly. He was put into a tent apart from the rest of the men, and only the doctor and camp steward, James Cummings, were allowed to see or attend him; but I went to see this man every day and nursed him. The last thing at night, I always went in to see that he was comfortable, but in spite of the good care and attention he received, he succumbed to the disease.

I was not in the least afraid of the small-pox. I had been vaccinated, and I drank sassafras tea constantly, which kept my blood purged and prevented me from contracting this dread scourge, and no one need fear getting it if they will only keep their blood in good condition with this sassafras tea, and take it before going where the patient is.

Notes on chapter *III.*

[1] This was a settlement on the southeast, ocean side of St. Simon's Island.

[2] A great number of Northern financial aid and missionary teachers were sent by the antislavery American Missionary Association to the Sea Islands soon after they were secured by the Union. Abolitionists hoped that this venture, called the Port Royal Experiment, would help to counter arguments of black inferiority by showing that the Negroes, if given the educational and cultural opportunity, would rise above the primitive life slavery imposed on them. Also, the missionaries hoped to make the freedmen's transition from slave to free status a smooth and successful one. Before the war ended, several hundred missionaries had come to the Sea Islands to teach the Negroes, and to help them operate the cotton plantations. With few exceptions, the U.S. Treasury agents and the Union troops stationed there remained antagonistic to these abolitionists. But their progress was followed closely in the North, particularly in Massachusetts where the antislavery cause was strongest, and in New York, where the American Missionary Association was headquartered. The Port Royal Experiment figured prominently in the abolitionist cause.

[3] Mansfield French was an energetic Methodist minister and educator who had been active in Ohio in earlier years. (He helped establish Wilberforce College, among others). In New York he raised funds for the American Missionary Association, and headed the first band of missionaries to come to the Sea Islands, in March, 1862.

[4] Liberia is, a republic in West Africa founded in 1822 by the American Colonization Society as a colony for freed slaves. Emigration, to Liberia or other areas, was thought by some to be the "solution" to the race problem. Advocates of this idea proposed gradual emancipation, followed by emigration. Slave holders, on the other hand, supported the Society because they felt that the presence of freedmen weakened the institution of slavery; they felt that all freedmen should be deported. It was often presumed that blacks would prefer to leave the country, but emigration was never a popular choice when the decision was actually faced.

[5] Of the first man killed in this skirmish Thomas Wentworth Higginson wrote, "He was probably the first black man who fell under arms in the war. . . . This was the first armed encounter, so far as I know, between the rebels and their former slaves." (Higginson's account, drawn from Trowbridge's testimony, has John Brown as the leader and first killed.) It was a

spontaneous, civilian action. The blacks were no doubt given confidence by the fact that their masters had earlier fled the island in fear. (Thomas P. Higginson, *Army Life in a Black Regiment* Boston, 1870, p. 274.)

⁶Susie's first husband whom she married in 1862. He was a sergeant in the First South Carolina Volunteers. *(See Introduction.)*

⁷Charles T. Trowbridge was a sergeant with the First South Carolina Volunteers, or "Hunter's Regiment" as it was called, a unit of black soldiers organized in May 1862, and disbanded in August, except for one company. Now acting as Captain, Trowbridge brought this company to St. Simon's with orders to hold and guard the newly taken island. The company had heard about the band of rebels and came ashore ready to fight them. They were greatly surprised to find that the islands' black inhabitants had taken the matter into their own hands. They joined forces, and together ousted the rebels.

⁸Hilton Head, one of the South Carolina Sea Islands, was the site of the Union's supply base for the blockade of the southern coast. General David Hunter, Commanding Officer of the Department of the South, was stationed at Hilton Head, and it was here that he directed the formation of the Union's first black troops in May, 1862. The First South Carolina Volunteers were officially reorganized and mustered into service in November, 1862.

⁹Mr. Hazzard himself was among these rebels. He wrote later of this skirmish in a letter to a friend, "If you wish to know hell before your time, go to St. Simon's and be hunted ten days by niggers." Ironically this letter was discovered among papers found by the First South Carolina Volunteers when they occupied Jacksonville in March, 1863. (Higginson, p. 275)

¹⁰The use of black troops caused outrage in the Confederacy. President Lincoln was accused on exciting servile war and Negro insurrection and the Confederate Congress issued orders that captured Negro soldiers and their officers were to be put to death. The Confederate soldiers kidnapped Negroes serving the Union and returned them to slavery, often after cruelly torturing them. In this way many slaves manumitted by their owners before the war were returned to slavery during the war. Knowing the fate that awaited them at Confederate hands gave the black soldiers reason to fight fiercely—they had much to lose if they were captured or if the Union should be defeated.

¹¹General David Hunter had been issuing emancipation or-

ders almost since the day of his appointment as Commander of the Department of the South, March 31, 1862. In May he declared martial law and freedom for all blacks in the Union-held territories whereupon he began organizing a unit of black troops. This news was joyfully received by abolitionists, who had long been fighting for the Negroes' right to join the army. But the issue was extremely controversial, even among loyal unionists, and President Lincoln rescinded Hunter's orders, both because they had been given without authority from the War Department, and because Hunter was interfering with the President's own plans for emancipation. On August 25, 1862, however, War Secretary Edwin M. Stanton authorized General Rufus Saxton, military governor of the region including South Carolina and Hunter's subordinate, to raise up to five regiments of black troops. In November Saxton offered Thomas Wentworth Higginson the colonelcy of the regiment. Higginson, then a Captain with the Fifty-First Massachusetts Regiment, was a natural choice. A long-time abolitionist, he had frequently voiced the hope that the Union would enlist blacks in the Army. Captain Charles T. Trowbridge was given charge of Company A of the regiment, comprised largely of men who had originally served under Hunter and who remained in the army through the months when its fate was uncertain.

[12]Standardized uniforms had been established by both the Confederate and the Union Armies, but some units had their own, distinctive, more colorful uniforms. The bright and rather exotic zouave uniforms described here were also adopted by a number of other Union regiments in the Civil War. Along with promises for equal pay and the issuance of Springfield rifles, the First South Carolina Volunteers had also been promised regulation Union "blues" by General Hunter.

[13]From the first the black soldiers had doubted they would get equal pay. They were discouraged by the fate of Hunter's Regiment, many of whose embittered members refused to reenlist in the new regiment; they were also discouraged by the many rumors and fears rampant in the new freedmen's encampments. Higginson wrote that he and other officers encouraged the men in their hope for pay, reading them the instructions of Secretary Stanton promising full pay. Eighteen months later, he noted, the officers were humiliated to admit that the troops' distrust had not been unwise, and the officers' "faith in the pledges of the United States Government . . . was foolishness." Appendix D of Higginson, "The Struggle for Pay" outlines some of the efforts he made to secure full pay for the black troops after his retirement from the regiment. (Higginson, pp. 16, 280)

[14]Varioloid—A form of small-pox.

# IV
# CAMP SAXTON—
# PROCLAMATION AND
# BARBECUE
# 1863

ON the first of January, 1863, we held services for the purpose of listening to the reading of President Lincoln's proclamation by Dr. W. H. Brisbane, and the presentation of two beautiful stands of colors, one from a lady in Connecticut, and the other from Rev. Mr. Cheever. The presentation speech was made by Chaplain French. It was a glorious day for us all, and we enjoyed every minute of it, and as a fitting close and the crowning event of this occasion we had a grand barbecue. A number of oxen were roasted whole, and we had a fine feast. Although not served as tastily or correctly as it would have been at home, yet it was enjoyed with keen appetites and relish. The soldiers had a good time. They sang or shouted "Hurrah!" all through the camp, and seemed overflowing with fun and frolic until taps were sounded, when many, no doubt, dreamt of this memorable day.[1]

I had rather an amusing experience; that is, it seems amusing now, as I look back, but at the time it occurred it was a most serious one to me. When our regiment left Beaufort for Seabrooke, I left some of my things with a neighbor who lived outside of the camp. After I had been at Seabrooke about a week, I decided to return to Camp Saxton and get them. So one morning, with Mary Shaw, a friend who was in the company at that time, I started off. There was no way for us to get to Beaufort other than to walk, except we rode on the commissary wagon. This we did, and reached Beaufort about one o'clock. We then had more than two miles to walk before reaching our old camp, and expected to be able to accomplish this and return in time to meet the wagon again by three o'clock that afternoon, and so be taken back. We failed to do this, however, for when we got to Beaufort the wagon was gone. We did not know what to do. I did not wish to remain overnight, neither did my friend, although we might easily have stayed, as both had relatives in the town.

It was in the springtime, and the days were long, and as the sun looked so bright, we concluded to walk back, thinking we should reach camp before dark. So off we started on our ten-mile tramp. We had not gone many miles, however, before we were all tired out and began to regret our undertaking. The sun was getting low, and we grew more frightened, fearful of meeting some animal or of treading on a snake on our way. We did not meet a person, and we were frightened almost to death. Our feet were so sore we could hardly walk. Finally we took off our shoes and tried walking in our stocking feet, but this made them worse. We had gone about six miles when night overtook us. There we were, nothing around us but dense woods, and as there was no house or any place to stop at, there was nothing for us to do but continue on. We were afraid to speak to each other.

Meantime at the camp, seeing no signs of us by dusk, they concluded we had decided to remain over until next day, and so had no idea of our plight. Imagine their surprise when we reached camp about eleven P.M. The guard challenged us, "Who comes there?" My answer was, "A friend without a countersign."[2] He approached and saw who it was, reported, and we were admitted into the lines. They had the joke on us that night, and for a long time after would tease us; and sometimes some of the men who were on guard that night would call us deserters. They used to laugh at us, but we joined with them too, especially when we would tell them our experience on our way to camp. I did not undertake that trip again, as there was no way of getting in or out except

one took the provision wagon, and there was
not much dependence to be put in that returning to camp. Perhaps the driver would say one
hour and he might be there earlier or later. Of
course it was not his fault, as it depended
when the order was filled at the Commissary
Department; therefore I did not go any more
until the regiment was ordered to our new
camp,[3] which was named after our hero, Colonel Shaw,[4] who at that time was at Beaufort
with his regiment, the 54th Massachusetts.[5]

I taught a great many of the comrades in
Company E to read and write, when they were
off duty. Nearly all were anxious to learn. My
husband taught some also when it was conve-
nient for him. I was very happy to know my
efforts were successful in camp, and also felt
grateful for the appreciation of my services. I
gave my services willingly for four years and
three months without receiving a dollar. I was
glad, however, to be allowed to go with the
regiment, to care for the sick and afflicted comrades.

Notes on chapter *IV.*

[1] The reader may want to read both Higginson's and Charlotte Forten's descriptions of the celebration of New Year's Day 1863, the day the Emancipation Proclamation took effect. (See Ray Allen Billington, *The Diary of Charlotte Forten,* New York, 1953)

[2] Countersign—a password, used for entry to the camp. The countersign changed daily, and guards turned away anyone not knowing it.

[3] The new camp on Port Royal Island, was described by Higginson as "very pleasantly situated, just out of [the town of] Beaufort. . . . Our first encampment [Camp Saxton] had been lower down that same river, and we felt at home." The regiment was ordered to Fort Shaw late in 1863. (Higginson, p. 224)

[4] This rugged and well-educated young man from a prominent Boston abolitionist family followed Higginson's lead in accepting the colonelcy of the first Northern Negro regiment, the Fifty-Fourth Massachusetts. Six weeks after the regiment's arrival at Beaufort from Boston, Colonel Robert Gould Shaw was killed leading the regiment's first major combat assignment, the unsuccessful assault on nearby Fort Wagner, July 18, 1863. In Chapter 1 of *The Negro in the Civil War,* Benjamin Quarles gives a stirring account of the heroic, black 54th Massachusetts Regiment and Colonel Shaw. A romantic and greatly admired figure in life, the young abolitionist was mourned throughout the Union in death; he had personified the Union's cause for freedom.

[5] Abolitionists in Massachusetts followed Colonel Higginson's reports from South Carolina very closely. Governor Andrews, especially, had been pressing President Lincoln to authorize more black regiments for the Union army. Finally, in January, 1863, word came that Massachusetts, which had already sent fifty-three regiments to fight the rebels, could organize its own black unit. It took two months to organize the Fifty-Fourth Massachusetts. In it were Negroes from every state and Canada, most of whom, unlike the Southern black troopers, had been free for some time—Frederick Douglass' two sons among them. The Fifty-Fourth's sendoff from Boston to Beaufort had the air of a crusade's farewell; the Negro troops symbolized the cause of justice to the crowds of Yankee liberals.

Once in South Carolina, the Fifty-Fourth's first battle assignment was one of the bloodiest battles of the war—in all nearly 1,700 soldiers were killed in the Union's unsuccessful attempt to take Fort Wagner, a battery protecting Charleston harbor. This encounter between Negro and Confederate troops swayed Union opinion regarding the armies of the Negroes. By the end of that year, sixty black units were being organized in various parts of the country.

# V
## MILITARY EXPEDITIONS,[1] AND LIFE IN CAMP


IN the latter part of 1862 the regiment made an expedition into Darien, Georgia, and up the Ridge, and on January 23, 1863, another up St. Mary's River,[2] capturing a number of stores for the government; then on to Fernandina, Florida. They were gone ten or twelve days, at the end of which time they returned to camp.

March 10, 1863, we were ordered to Jacksonville,[3] Florida. Leaving Camp Saxton between four and five o'clock, we arrived at Jacksonville about eight o'clock next morning, accompanied by three or four gunboats. When the rebels saw these boats, they ran out of the city, leaving the women behind, and we found out afterwards that they thought we had a much larger fleet than we really had. Our regiment was kept out of sight until we made fast at the wharf where it landed, and while the gunboats were shelling[4] up the river and as far inland as possible, the regiment landed and marched up the street, where they spied the rebels who had fled from the city. They were hiding behind a house about a mile or so away, their faces blackened to disguise themselves as negroes, and our boys, as they advanced toward them, halted a second, saying, "They are black men! Let them come to us, or we will make them know who we are." With this, the firing was opened and several of our men were wounded and killed. The rebels had a number wounded and killed. It was through this way the discovery was made that they were white men. Our men drove them some distance in retreat and then threw out their pickets.[5]

While the fighting was on, a friend, Lizzie Lancaster, and I stopped at several of the rebel homes, and after talking with some of the women and children we asked them if they had any food. They claimed to have only some hard-tack,[6] and evidently did not care to give us anything to eat, but this was not surprising. They were bitterly against our people and had no mercy or sympathy for us.[7]

The second day, our boys were reinforced by a regiment of white soldiers,[8] a Maine regiment, and by cavalry, and had quite a fight. On the third day, Edward Herron, who was a fine gunner on the steamer John Adams, came on shore, bringing a small cannon,[9] which the men pulled along for more than five miles. This cannon was the only piece for shelling.

On coming upon the enemy, all secured their
places, and they had a lively fight, which
lasted several hours, and our boys were nearly
captured by the Confederates; but the Union
boys carried out all their plans that day, and
succeeded in driving the enemy back. After
this skirmish, every afternoon between four
and five o'clock the Confederate General
Finegan would send a flag of truce to Colonel
Higginson, warning him to send all women
and children out of the city, and threatening to
bombard it if this was not done. Our colonel
allowed all to go who wished, at first, but as
General Finegan grew more hostile and kept
sending these communications for nearly a
week, Colonel Higginson thought it not best or
necessary to send any more out of the city, and
so informed General Finegan. This angered
the general, for that night the rebels shelled
directly toward Colonel Higginson's headquarters. The shelling was so heavy that the colonel
told my captain to have me taken up into the
town to a hotel, which was used as a hospital.
As my quarters were just in the rear of the
colonel's, he was compelled to leave his also
before the night was over. I expected every
moment to be killed by a shell, but on arriving
at the hospital I knew I was safe, for the shells
could not reach us there. It was plainly to be
seen now, the ruse of the flag of truce coming
so often to us. The bearer was evidently a spy
getting the location of the headquarters, etc.,

for the shells were sent too accurately to be at random.

Next morning Colonel Higginson took the cavalry and a regiment on another tramp after the rebels. They were gone several days and had the hardest fight they had had, for they wanted to go as far as a station which was some distance from the city. The gunboats were of little assistance to them, yet notwithstanding this drawback our boys returned with only a few killed and wounded, and after this we were not troubled with General Finegan.

We remained here a few weeks longer, when, about April first, the regiment was ordered back[10] to Camp Saxton, where it stayed a week, when the order came to go to Port Royal Ferry[11] on picket duty.[12] It was a gay day for the boys. By seven o'clock all tents were down, and each company, with a commissary wagon, marched up the shell road, which is a beautiful avenue ten or twelve miles out of Beaufort. We arrived at Seabrooke at about four o'clock, where our tents were pitched and the men put on duty. We were here a few weeks, when Company E was ordered to Barnwell plantation[13] for picket duty.

Some mornings I would go along the picket line, and I could see the rebels on the opposite side of the river. Sometimes as they were changing pickets they would call over to our men and ask for something to eat, or for tobacco, and our men would tell them to come

**Thomas Wentworth Higginson**
Colonel First South Carolina Volunteers
*Afterwards 33d U.S.C.T.*

over. Sometimes one or two would desert to us, saying, they "had no negroes to fight for."[14] Others would shoot across at our picket, but as the river was so wide there was never any damage done, and the Confederates never attempted to shell us while we were there.

I learned to handle a musket very well while in the regiment, and could shoot straight and often hit the target. I assisted in cleaning the guns and used to fire them off, to see if the cartridges were dry, before cleaning and reloading, each day. I thought this great fun. I was also able to take a gun all apart, and put it together again.

Between Barnwell and the mainland was Hall Island. I went over there several times with Sergeant King[15] and other comrades. One night there was a stir in camp when it was found that the rebels were trying to cross, and next morning Lieutenant Parker told me he thought they were on Hall Island; so after that I did not go over again.

While planning for the expedition up the Edisto River,[16] Colonel Higginson was a whole night in the water, trying to locate the rebels and where their picket lines were situated. About July the boys went up the Edisto to destroy a bridge on the Charleston and Savannah road.[17] This expedition was twenty or more miles into the mainland. Colonel Higginson was wounded in this fight and the regiment nearly captured. The steamboat John

Adams always assisted us, carrying soldiers, provisions, etc. She carried several guns and a good gunner, Edward Herron. Henry Batchlott, a relative of mine, was a steward on this boat. There were two smaller boats, Governor Milton and the Enoch Dean, in the fleet, as these could go up the river better than the larger ones could. I often went aboard the John Adams. It went with us into Jacksonville, to Cole and Folly Island, and Gunner Herron was always ready to send a shell at the enemy.

One night, Companies K and E, on their way to Pocotaligo[18] to destroy a battery that was situated down the river, captured several prisoners.[19] The rebels nearly captured Sergeant King, who, as he sprang and caught a "reb," fell over an embankment. In falling he did not release his hold on his prisoner. Although his hip was severely injured, he held fast until some of his comrades came to his aid and pulled them up. These expeditions were very dangerous. Sometimes the men had to go five or ten miles during the night over on the rebel side and capture or destroy whatever they could find.

While at Camp Shaw, there was a deserter who came into Beaufort. He was allowed his freedom about the city and was not molested. He remained about the place a little while and returned to the rebels again. On his return to Beaufort a second time, he was held as a spy, tried, and sentenced to death, for he was a traitor. The day he was shot, he was placed on a hearse with his coffin inside, a guard was placed either side of the hearse, and he was driven through the town. All the soldiers and people in town were out, as this was to be a warning to the soldiers. Our regiment was in line on dress parade. They drove with him to the rear of our camp, where he was shot. I shall never forget this scene.

While at Camp Shaw, Chaplain Fowler, Robert Defoe, and several of our boys were captured while tapping some telegraph wires. Robert Defoe was confined in jail[20] at Walterborough, S.C., for about twenty months. When Sherman's army reached Pocotaligo he made his escape and joined his company (Company G). He had not been paid, as he had refused the reduced pay offered by the government. Before we got to camp, where the pay-rolls could be made out, he sickened and died of small-pox, and was buried at Savannah, never having been paid one cent for nearly three years of service. He left no heirs and his account was never settled.

In winter, when it was very cold, I would take a mess-pan, put a little earth in the bottom, and go to the cook-shed and fill it nearly full of coals, carry it back to my tent and put another pan over it; so when the provost guard went through camp after taps, they would not see the light, as it was against the rules to have a light after taps. In this way I was heated and kept very warm.

A mess-pan is made of sheet iron, some-thing like our roasting pans, only they are nearly as large round as a peck measure, but not so deep. We had fresh beef once in a while, and we would have soup, and the vegetables they put in this soup were dried and pressed. They looked like hops. Salt beef was our stand-by. Sometimes the men would have what we called slap-jacks. This was flour, made into bread and spread thin on the bottom of the mess-pan to cook. Each man had one of them, with a pint of tea, for his supper, or a pint of tea and five or six hard-tack. I often got my own meals, and would fix some dishes for the non-commissioned officers also.

Mrs. Chamberlain, our quartermaster's wife, was with us here. She was a beautiful woman; I can see her pleasant face before me now, as she, with Captain Trowbridge, would sit and converse with me in my tent two or three hours at a time. She was also with me on Cole Island, and I think we were the only women with the regiment while there. I remember well how, when she first came into camp, Cap-tain Trowbridge brought her to my tent and introduced her to me. I found her then, as she remained ever after, a lovely person, and I always admired her cordial and friendly ways.

Our boys would say to me sometimes, "Mrs. King, why is it you are so kind to us? You treat us just as you do the boys in your own com-

Major H. A. Whitney            Lieut. J. B. West
                Henry Batchlott
          Steward of the John Adams

pany." I replied, "Well, you know, all the boys in other companies are the same to me as those in my Company E; you are all doing the same duty, and I will do just the same for you." "Yes," they would say, "we know that, because you were the first woman we saw when we came into camp, and you took an interest in us boys ever since we have been here, and we are very grateful for all you do for us."

When at Camp Shaw, I visited the hospital in Beaufort, where I met Clara Barton.[21] There were a number of sick and wounded soldiers there, and I went often to see the comrades. Miss Barton was always very cordial toward me, and I honored her for her devotion and care for those men.

There was a man, John Johnson, who with his family was taken by our regiment at Edisto. This man afterwards worked in the hospital and was well known to Miss Barton. I have been told since that when she went South, in 1883, she tried to look this man up, but learned he was dead. His son is living in Edisto, Rev. J. J. Johnson, and is the president of an industrial school on that island and a very intelligent man. He was a small child when his father and family were captured by our regiment at Edisto.

Notes on chapter *V*.

[1] The purposes of the first of these expeditions, writes Dudley P. Cornish, "were to feel out the rebel picket lines along the coasts of Florida and Georgia . . . to destroy saltworks and whatever food and supplies could not be taken off, and to bring in whatever slaves could be found. There was one other important purpose: Saxton wanted to find out what the fighting qualities of his troops actually were," although the regiment was far from complete both in numbers and training.

From November 3 to 10, 1862, the black soldiers of Company A, aboard a captured steamer, "spread havoc along the coast of Georgia and Northern Florida. They drove in rebel pickets at point after point, killed nine of the enemy, took three prisoners, destroyed nine different saltworks [and] $20,000 worth of . . . Confederate property, and they carried off over one hundred and fifty slaves." Only four men were wounded. Their commander reported, "I started from Saint Simon's island with sixty-two colored fighting men and returned to Beaufort with 156 fighting men (all colored). As soon as we took a slave from his claimant, we placed a musket in his hand and he began to fight for the freedom of the others."

General Saxton was overjoyed at the success of his troops, and wrote to the Secretary of War that "the Negroes fought with a coolness and bravery that would have done credit to veteran soldiers. There was no excitement, no flinching, no attempt at cruelty when successful. They seemed like men who were fighting to vindicate their manhood, and they did it well." This and the following expeditions received national publicity, and greatly aided the abolitionists' demands for arming Negroes.

The following expeditions were made for the purpose of getting badly needed building supplies. Lumber was shipped to the Union forces from the North, even though the South was full of timber, but all of it in rebel-held territory. In most cases, slaves flocked to the approaching Union forces for safety and liberation. The army helped to evacuate thousands to Union-held territories, and continued to recruit new troops from the ranks of the refugees. (Dudley P. Cornish, *The Sable Arm* pp. 85–88, New York, 1966)

[2] The St. Mary's expedition was the First South Carolina Volunteers' initial assignment under Colonel Higginson. He had been anxious to get his men into battle, for the world was watching this experiment in black soldiering, and skeptics still said the former slaves would be cowardly and flinching under

fire. St. Mary's proved otherwise. The battle which took place there was reported in many contemporary newspapers, and Higginson's own report was widely read. (In 1865 it appeared in the *Atlantic*.) Again, this caused increasing demands from the North for the formation of new Negro fighting units.

[3] The instructions for this expedition, ordered by General Saxton, (Military Governor of the Department of the South) read in part, "I expect . . . that you will occupy Jacksonville, Florida, and intrench yourselves there.

"The main objects of your expedition are to carry the proclamation of freedom to the enslaved; to call all loyal men into the service of the United States; to occupy as much of the State of Florida as possible with the forces under your command; and to neglect no means consistent with the usages of civilized warfare to weaken, harass, and annoy those who are in rebellion against the Government of the United States." (Higginson, pp. 99–100)

[4] Shelling—Bombarding with cannon.

[5] The regiment sent out a detachment of guards. Pickets, or guards, were used to protect against enemy raiders and to hold the lines gained by fighting.

[6] Hard-tack—A hard bread, something like Southern beaten biscuits, used in times of travel or scarce rations because it kept well. It was also a mainstay of the cowboys and Western pioneers for the same reasons.

[7] This contradicts Higginson, who reported that the whites in Florida professed to have union sentiments, but that the blacks found this attitude insincere and hypocritical.

[8] Two regiments arrived March 20–21, 1863, the Sixth Connecticut and the Eighth Maine. Higginson had been longing for these reinforcements, because his men were so tired and battle weary from this and the previous expeditions. When the Yankee soldiers arrived he wrote in his diary (March 20, 1863), "I only wish they were black; but now I have to show, not only that blacks can fight, but that they and white soldiers can act in harmony together." Later he added to his reminiscences, "It was the first time in the war (so far as I know) that white and black soldiers had served together on regular duty. Jealousy was still felt towards even the officers of the colored regiments, and any difficult contingency would be apt to bring it out. . . . The first twelve hours of this mixed command were to me a

more anxious period than any outward alarms had created."
(Higginson, pp. 117–118)

[9]This gun (a ten-pound Parrott) was mounted on a railroad
handcar. The troops advanced along the tracks with it, even-
tually meeting a similarly mounted cannon (a 264-pound
Blakeley) of the enemy's, judged to be two miles away.

The rebel's gun, being much larger, inflicted greater damage
than the small Union gun. But the Union forces held their
own, and before returning to Jacksonville they advanced far-
ther along the railway to remove a section of the track, thus
preventing the rebels from bringing their cannon near the city.

[10]The orders to evacuate Jacksonville came as a complete
surprise. The Union forces had hardly begun to carry out the
orders which had sent them there. The men were extremely
disappointed to have their expedition cut short. Higginson
proposed two theories to account for the evacuation orders: it
was a means of cutting short the career of the black troops (he
attributes this to Hunter's proslavery advisors), or, the army
sensed that too few soldiers had been sent to hold Jacksonville,
since the next expedition was ordered there the following year
with twenty thousand men, in contrast to the two thousand
men in this expedition. Earlier Higginson had puzzled over
the fact that the Eighth Maine arrived with only enough rations to last ten days.

Rose and Cornish assert, however, that the units were recalled
from Jacksonville simply to make ready for the War Department's projected assault on Charleston.

[11]"The only thoroughfare by land between Beaufort and
Charleston is the 'Shell Road,' a beautiful avenue, which,
about nine miles from Beaufort, strikes a ferry across the
Coosaw River. War abolished the ferry, and made the river the
permanent barrier between the opposing picket lines." "This
picket station was regarded as a sort of military picnic by the
regiments stationed at Beaufort . . . [and by] the colored soldiers especially, with their love of country life, and their exten-
sive personal acquaintance on the plantations. . . . [I]t was
something to dwell on the Coosaw." (Higginson, pp. 130–131,
134–135)

[12]This was at the time of a Union offensive against Charleston,
and it was thought that the Confederates would try to recap-
ture the Sea Islands from their mainland posts.

[13] "[O]ld Beaufort and its vicinity were the seedbed of South Carolina secessionism. . . . The mansions of the . . . Barnwells, and the Seabrooks stood abandoned among their stately live oaks and festoons of Spanish moss. . . . The old masters had vanished quickly and completely. . . ." (C. Vann Woodward in Willie Lee Rose, *Rehearsal for Reconstruction*, Baltimore, 1964, p. xv)

[14] The rebels meant that they, not owning any slaves, had no reason to be fighting for the cause of slavery.

[15] This is Edward King, Susie King's husband.

[16] The Edisto flows through South Carolina and out to sea by Edisto Island, which lies about halfway between Port Royal Island and Charleston. Along the Edisto's south fork, or Pon-Pon River, were many rice plantations worked by slaves.

[17] Higginson wrote that General Gillmore, Hunter's replacement as commander of the Department of the South, considered this expedition up the Edisto as one of three major points in the Union's "siege of Charleston." But Higginson himself disputed this, saying it had been planned first by the officers of the First South Carolina Volunteers, based on facts learned from their men. Thirty miles up the Edisto, they estimated, was the bulk of the slave population which had been withdrawn from the coastal plantations by their owners when the Union captured the Sea Islands.

Since there were two railway routes between Charleston and Savannah, destroying a bridge on one of them would simply harass the enemy at best. But the officers of the First South Carolina had pursued the plan, hoping to achieve the now secondary objective of freeing slaves and recruiting new black troops along the way.

They were, in fact, unsuccessful in destroying the bridge, but freed two hundred slaves, causing Higginson to write, ". . . I know that the day was worth all it cost, and more." (Higginson, pp. 167, 184)

[18] Pocotaligo—A town on the mainland, about fifteen miles up the Coosaw River from Port Royal Island.

[19] Higginson reported that on the excursion toward Pocotaligo some rebel pickets were captured, and all the slaves of one plantation were brought away—"the latter operation

being entirely under the charge of Sergeant Harry Williams (Company K) without the presence of any white man." The rebels had with them a pack of bloodhounds trained to run down fugitive slaves. The men from Company K managed to kill some of these dogs—they were fearful reminders of their years in slavery." (Higginson, pp. 230–231)

[20] Chaplain Fowler was also held as prisoner of war, an act contrary to war agreements made by both sides. Defoe, wrote Higginson, "did not know, nor did any of us know, whether he would be treated as a prisoner of war, or shot, or sent to a rice plantation," so unpredictable was the rebel treatment of Negro soldiers. (Higginson, p. 28)

[21] Clara Barton (1821–1912), founder of the American Red Cross and often called America's Florence Nightingale, was a white nurse to Civil War soldiers. Clara Barton had nursed the soldiers after the Fort Wagner massacre: " 'I can see again,' " she later wrote, " 'the scarlet flow of blood as it rolled over the black limbs beneath my hands . . .' " "Oftentimes as Mrs. Barton made the rounds in the hospital during her eight months in the Sea Islands, she was accompanied by Susie King, whom [sic] she treated with cordiality." (Benjamin Quarles, *Negroes in the Civil War*, Boston, 1955, pp. 16, 228)

A slave auction in the South

A slave auction in the South

Blacks unloading boats for the Union Army

Freed Blacks working on Sea Island plantations

Recruiting poster for Black regiments

Black soldiers taking their oath of allegiance to the
United States.

Black recruits training for combat

Blacks receiving full pay for their service as soldiers
after the Enrollment Act of March 3, 1865

The 54th Massachusetts leading the attack as the Union
forces storm Fort Wagner

The 2nd South Carolina Volunteers raiding the rice
plantations on the Combahee River in South Carolina

Schools for children and adults beginning to develop in
and around the Union Army camps after various
churches send books from the North

North Union officers as the responsible agents in
schools for soldiers and freemen

Reign of Terror over the newly-freed slaves (Scene from
Memphis Tennessee)

# VI
# ON MORRIS AND OTHER ISLANDS

FORT WAGNER being only a mile from our camp, I went there two or three times a week, and would go up on the ramparts to watch the gunners send their shells into Charleston (which they did every fifteen minutes), and had a full view of the city from that point. Outside of the fort were many skulls lying about; I have often moved them one side out of the path. The comrades and I would have quite a debate as to which side the men fought on. Some thought that they were the skulls of our boys; others thought they were the enemy's; but as there was no definite way to know, it was never decided which could lay claim to them. They were a gruesome sight, those fleshless heads and grinning jaws, but by this time I had become accustomed to worse things and did not feel as I might have earlier in my camp life.

It seems strange how our aversion to seeing

suffering is overcome in war,—how we are able
to see the most sickening sights, such as men
with their limbs blown off and mangled by the
deadly shells, without a shudder; and instead
of turning away, how we hurry to assist in
alleviating their pain, bind up their wounds,
and press the cool water to their parched lips,
with feelings only of sympathy and pity.

About the first of June, 1864, the regiment
was ordered to Folly Island,[1] staying there until the latter part of the month, when it was
ordered to Morris Island. We landed on Morris
Island between June and July, 1864. This island
was a narrow strip of sandy soil, nothing growing on it but a few bushes and shrubs. The
camp was one mile from the boat landing,
called Pawnell Landing, and the landing one
mile from Fort Wagner.

Colonel Higginson had left us in May of this
year, on account of wounds received at Edisto.
All the men were sorry to lose him.[2] They did
not want him to go, they loved him so. He was
kind and devoted to his men, thoughtful for
their comfort, and we missed his genial presence from the camp.

The regiment under Colonel Trowbridge[3]
did garrison duty, but they had troublesome
times from Fort Gregg, on James Island, for the
rebels would throw a shell over on our island
every now and then. Finally orders were received for the boys to prepare to take Fort
Gregg, each man to take 150 rounds of car-

tridges, canteens of water, hard-tack, and salt beef. This order was sent three days prior to starting, to allow them to be in readiness. I helped as many as I could to pack haversacks and cartridge boxes.

The fourth day, about five o'clock in the afternoon, the call was sounded, and I heard the first sergeant say, "Fall in, boys, fall in," and they were not long obeying the command. Each company marched out of its street, in front of their colonel's headquarters, where they rested for half an hour, as it was not dark enough, and they did not want the enemy to have a chance to spy their movements. At the end of this time the line was formed with the 103d New York (white) in the rear, and off they started, eager to get to work. It was quite dark by the time they reached Pawnell Landing. I have never forgotten the good-bys of that day, as they left camp. Colonel Trowbridge said to me as he left, "Good-by, Mrs. King, take care of yourself if you don't see us again." I went with them as far as the landing, and watched them until they got out of sight, and then I returned to the camp. There was no one at camp but those left on picket and a few disabled soldiers, and one woman, a friend of mine, Mary Shaw, and it was lonesome and sad, now that the boys were gone, some never to return.

Mary Shaw shared my tent that night, and we went to bed, but not to sleep, for the fleas nearly ate us alive. We caught a few, but it did seem now that the men were gone, that every flea in camp had located my tent, and caused us to vacate. Sleep being out of the question, we sat up the remainder of the night.

About four o'clock, July 2, the charge was made. The firing could be plainly heard in camp. I hastened down to the landing and remained there until eight o'clock that morning. When the wounded arrived, or rather began to arrive, the first one brought in was Samuel Anderson of our company. He was badly wounded. Then others of our boys, some with their legs off, arm gone, foot off, and wounds of all kinds imaginable. They had to wade through creeks and marshes, as they were discovered by the enemy and shelled very badly. A number of the men were lost, some got fastened in the mud and had to cut off the legs of their pants, to free themselves. The 103d New York suffered the most, as their men were very badly wounded.

My work now began. I gave my assistance to try to alleviate their sufferings. I asked the doctor at the hospital what I could get for them to eat. They wanted soup, but that I could not get; but I had a few cans of condensed milk and some turtle eggs, so I thought I would try to make some custard. I had doubts as to my success, for cooking with turtle eggs was something new to me, but the adage has it, "Nothing ventured, nothing done," so I made a venture and the result was a very delicious custard. This I carried to the men, who enjoyed it very much. My services were given at all times for the comfort of these men. I was on hand to assist whenever needed. I was enrolled as company laundress, but I did very little of it, because I was always busy doing other things through camp, and was employed all the time doing something for the officers and comrades.

After this fight, the regiment did not return to the camp for one month. They were ordered to Cole Island in September, where they remained until October. About November 1, 1864, six companies were detailed to go to Gregg Landing, Port Royal Ferry, and the rebels in some way found out some of our forces had been removed and gave our boys in camp a hard time of it, for several nights. In fact, one night it was thought the boys would have to retreat. The colonel told me to go down to the landing, and if they were obliged to retreat, I could go aboard one of our gunboats. One of the gunboats got in the rear, and began to shell General Beauregard's force, which helped our boys retain their possession.

About November 15, I received a letter from Sergeant King, saying the boys were still lying three miles from Gregg Landing and had not had a fight yet; that the rebels were waiting on them and they on the rebels, and each were holding their own; also that General Sherman had taken Fort McAllister, eight miles from Savannah. After receiving this letter I wanted to get to Beaufort, so I could be near to them and so be able to get news from my husband. November 23 I got a pass for Beaufort. I arrived at Hilton Head about three o'clock next day, but there had been a battle, and a steamer arrived with a number of wounded men; so I could not get a transfer to Beaufort. The doctor wished me to remain over until Monday. I did not want to stay. I was anxious to get off, as I knew no one at Hilton Head.

I must mention a pet pig we had on Cole Island. Colonel Trowbridge brought into camp, one day, a poor, thin little pig, which a German soldier brought back with him on his return from a furlough. His regiment, the 74th Pennsylvania, was just embarking for the North, where it was ordered to join the 10th corps, and he could not take the pig back with him, so he gave it to our colonel. That pig grew to be the pet of the camp, and was the special care of the drummer boys, who taught him many tricks; and so well did they train him that every day at practice and dress parade, his pigship would march out with them, keeping perfect time with their music. The drummers would often disturb the devotions by riding this pig into the midst of evening praise meeting, and many were the complaints made to the colonel, but he was always very lenient toward the boys, for he knew they only did this for mis-

Lieut. John A. Trowbridge
Lieut. Eli C. Merriam        Lieut. James M. Thompson
Lieut. Jerome T. Furman

chief. I shall never forget the fun we had in camp with "Piggie."

Notes on chapter *VI.*

[1] The regiment remained headquartered on these islands near Charleston during the close of Sherman's decisive and destructive march to the sea, when Savannah was taken (December 22, 1864) and on into February, 1865. Higginson wrote that the black troops' maintenance of the picket lines alongside the Coosaw River insured the Union's foothold on the islands, "and upon that again finally depended the whole campaign of Sherman. But for the services of the colored troops, which finally formed the main garrison of the Department of the South, the Great March would never have been performed." (Higginson, p. 135)

[2] Under Higginson's colonelcy, thousands of slaves had been liberated and flocked to the islands, deserting inland plantations. Able men were enlisted as Union troops, the remaining freedmen settling in new towns on the islands. They named one of these settlements Higginsonville in honor of their liberator. Higginson's dedication to the abolitionist cause, his enthusiasm for his appointment with the First South Carolina Volunteers, his affection for and loyalty to his regiment—all of these made his forced resignation a sad occasion for him. His report from the South, and later, his reminiscences were widely read in the North, and very influential in the cause for equality. After his retirement, Higginson publicly crusaded for equal pay for the black troops until it was granted.

[3] Colonel W. T. Bennett officially took charge of the regiment after Colonel Higginson's departure, but it was Lt. Colonel Charles T. Trowbridge who in fact commanded the regiment until the end of the war. As a young army engineer under General Hunter, Sergeant Trowbridge had helped organize the unit and as a lieutenant he had commanded the little band of ex-slaves (Company "A") who comprised the First South Carolina Volunteers before its official reinstatement in November, 1862. Trowbridge retired from the regiment in 1865, as Lieutenant Colonel. Like Higginson, he was greatly admired by his troops, perhaps even more so, as Mrs. Taylor suggests. This may be partly due to his continuity of tenure, and his refusal to leave the troops at the end of his three-year tour of duty, both of which must have greatly endeared him to his men.

# VII
## CAST AWAY

THERE was a yacht that carried passengers from Hilton Head to Beaufort. There were also five small boats which carried people over. The only people here, besides the soldiers, were Mrs. Lizzie Brown, who came over on a permit to see her husband, who was at this place, and was very ill (he died while she was there), Corporal Walker's wife, with her two years old child, and Mrs. Seabrooke. As soon as we could get the yacht, these persons I have mentioned, together with a comrade just discharged, an officer's boy, and myself, took passage on it for Beaufort. It was nearly dark before we had gone any distance, and about eight o'clock we were cast away and were only saved through the mercy of God. I remember going down twice. As I rose the second time, I caught hold of the sail and managed to hold fast. Mrs. Walker held on to her child with one hand, while with the other she managed to hold fast to some part of the boat, and we drifted and shouted as loud as we could, trying to attract the attention of some of the government boats which were going up and down the river. But it was in vain, we could not make ourselves heard, and just when we gave up all hope, and in the last moment (as we thought) gave one more despairing cry, we were heard at Ladies' Island. Two boats were put off and a search was made, to locate our distressed boat. They found us at last, nearly dead from exposure. In fact, the poor little baby was dead, although her mother still held her by her clothing, with her teeth. The soldier was drowned, having been caught under the sail and pinned down. The rest of us were saved. I had to be carried bodily, as I was thoroughly exhausted. We were given the best attention that we could get at this place where we were picked up. The men who saved us were surprised when they found me among the passengers, as one of them, William Geary, of Darien, Georgia, was a friend of my husband. His mother lived about two miles from where we were picked up, and she told me she had heard cries for a long time that night, and was very uneasy about it. Finally, she said to her son, "I think some poor souls are cast away." "I don't think so, mother," he replied; "I saw some people going down the river to-day. You know this is Christmas, and they are having a good time." But she still persisted that these were cries of distress, and not of joy, and begged him to go out and see. So to satisfy her, he went outside and listened, and then he heard them also, and hastened to get the boats off to find us. We were capsized about 8.15 P.M. and it was near midnight when they found us. Next day, they kept a sharp lookout on the beach for anything that might be washed in from the yacht, and got a trunk and several other things. Had the tide been going out, we should have been carried to sea and lost.

I was very ill and under the doctor's care for some time, in Beaufort. The doctor said I ought to have been rolled,[1] as I had swallowed so much water. In January, 1865, I went back to Cole Island, where I could be attended by my doctor, Dr. Miner, who did all in his power to alleviate my suffering, for I was swollen very much. This he reduced and I recovered, but had a severe cough for a long time afterward.

Notes on chapter *VII.*

[1] Victims of water exposure are sometimes rolled back and forth over a barrel or curved surface to bring up swallowed water.

# VIII
## A FLAG OF TRUCE

In October, 1864, six companies of the regiment were ordered to Gregg Landing, S. C. Captain L. W. Metcalf, of Co. G, was appointed on General Saxton's staff as provost captain, Lieutenant James B. West acting as assistant general. As in some way our mail had been sent over to the Confederate side and their mail to us, Captain Metcalf and Lieutenant West were detailed to exchange these letters under a flag of truce. So, with an escort of six men of the companies at Port Royal Ferry, the flag was unfurled and the message shouted across the river to the Confederates. Captain Metcalf asked them to come over to our side under the protection of our flag of truce. This the Confederates refused to do, having for their excuse that their boat was too far up the river and so they had no way to cross the river to us. They asked Metcalf to cross to them. He at once ordered his men to "stack arms,"[1] the

Confederates following suit, and his boys in blue rowed him over, and he delivered the message, after having introduced himself to the rebel officers. One of these officers was Major Jones, of Alabama, the other Lieutenant Scott, of South Carolina. Major Jones was very cordial to our captain, but Lieutenant Scott would not extend his hand, and stood aside, in sullen silence, looking as if he would like to take revenge then and there. Major Jones said to Captain Metcalf, "We have no one to fight for.[2] Should I meet you again, I shall not forget we have met before." With this he extended his hand to Metcalf and bade him good-by, but Lieutenant Scott stood by and looked as cross as he possibly could. The letters were exchanged, but it seemed a mystery just how those letters got missent to the opposite sides. Captain Metcalf said he did not feel a mite comfortable while he was on the Confederate soil; as for his men, you can imagine their thoughts. I asked them how they felt on the other side, and they said, "We would have felt much better if we had had our guns with us." It was a little risky, for sometimes the flag of truce is not regarded, but even among the enemy there are some good and loyal persons.

Captain Metcalf is [i.e., in 1902] still living in Medford. He is seventy-one years old, and just as loyal to the old flag and the G. A. R. as he was from 1861 to 1866, when he was mustered out. He was a brave captain, a good officer,

Capt. L. W. Metcalf
Capt. Miron W. Saxton                    Capt. A. W. Jackson
Corporal Peter Waggall

and was honored and beloved by all in the regiment.

Notes on chapter *VIII*.

[1] In this standard military procedure, rifles are hooked together in groups of three or more to stand upright, making a cone. This prevents the men from using their arms, assuring the other side of a temporary truce.

[2] Major Jones presumably meant that the Confederates had lost so many of their families and slaves that their morale was too low to promote vigorous fighting.

# IX
# CAPTURE OF CHARLESTON

ON February 28, 1865, the remainder of the regiment were ordered to Charleston, as there were signs of the rebels evacuating that city.[1] Leaving Cole Island, we arrived in Charleston between nine and ten o'clock in the morning, and found the "rebs" had set fire to the city and fled, leaving women and children behind to suffer and perish in the flames. The fire had been burning fiercely for a day and night. When we landed, under a flag of truce, our regiment went to work assisting the citizens in subduing the flames. It was a terrible scene. For three or four days the men fought the fire, saving the property and effects of the people, yet these white men and women could not tolerate our black Union soldiers, for many of them had formerly been their slaves; and although these brave men risked life and limb to assist them in their distress, men and even women would sneer and molest them whenever they met them.

I had quarters assigned me at a residence on South Battery Street, one of the most aristocratic parts of the city, where I assisted in caring for the sick and injured comrades. After getting the fire under control, the regiment marched out to the race track, where they camped until March 12, when we were ordered to Savannah, Ga. We arrived there on the 13th, about eight o'clock in the evening, and marched out to Fairlong, near the A. & G. R. R., where we remained about ten days, when we were ordered to Augusta, Ga., where Captain Alexander Heasley, of Co. E, was shot and killed by a Confederate. After his death Lieutenant Parker was made captain of the company, and was with us until the regiment was mustered out. He often told me about Massachusetts, but I had no thought at that time that I should ever see that State, and stand in the "Cradle of Liberty."

The regiment remained in Augusta for thirty days, when it was ordered to Hamburg, S. C., and then on to Charleston. It was while on their march through the country, to the latter city, that they came in contact with the bushwhackers[2] (as the rebels were called), who hid in the bushes and would shoot the Union boys every chance they got. Other times they would conceal themselves in the cars used to transfer our soldiers, and when our boys, worn out and tired, would fall asleep, these men would come out from their hiding places and cut their throats. Several of our men were killed in this way, but it could not be found out who was committing these murders until one night one of the rebels was caught in the act, trying to cut the throat of a sleeping soldier. He was put under guard, court-martialed, and shot at Wall Hollow.

First Lieutenant Jerome T. Furman and a number of soldiers were killed by these South Carolina bushwackers at Wall Hollow. After this man was shot, however, the regiment marched through unmolested to Charleston.

## Notes on chapter *IX*.

[1] Sherman's great march through Georgia to the coast and up through South Carolina was finished in December 1864 and the early months of 1865. Sherman specifically omitted Charleston from his path, feeling that its isolation would cause its fall. General Hardee, commander of the Confederate army in Georgia and South Carolina, ordered that the city be evacuated and, in order to leave as little as possible for the Union troops, he ordered it burned—including all ships and boats in the harbor. The mayor of Charleston readily surrendered to Lt. Colonel A. G. Bennett of the Twenty-first U.S. Colored Troops, who promised the assistance of the black men to the stricken people. The irony of this scene—the freed slaves now coming as victorious soldiers to the aid of the defeated, their old masters, makes one of the most poignant stories of the Civil War. "Some of them," writes Benjamin Quarles, "found themselves in the shadow of the auction block of J. B. Baker, on which they had once stood as chattels."

[2] Although the war was now over, Lee having surrendered to Grant at Appomattox on April 9, Sherman's march through South Carolina intensified the rebels' hatred for Union troops—a feeling which was not ruled by the conventions of warfare and truce.

# X
## MUSTERED OUT

THE regiment, under Colonel Trowbridge, reached Charleston in November, 1865, and camped on the race track until January, when they returned to Morris Island, and on February 9, 1866, the following "General Orders" were received and the regiment mustered out.

They were delighted to go home, but oh! how they hated to part from their commanding chief, Colonel C. T. Trowbridge. He was the very first officer to take charge of black soldiers. We thought there was no one like him, for he was a "man" among his soldiers. All in the regiment knew him personally, and many were the jokes he used to tell them. I shall never forget his friendship and kindness toward me, from the first time I met him to the end of the war. There was never any one from the North who came into our camp but he would bring them to see me.

While on a visit South in 1888, I met a comrade of the regiment, who often said to me,

"You up North, Mrs. King, do you ever see Colonel Trowbridge? How I should like to see him! I don't see why he does not come South sometime. Why, I would take a day off and look up all the 'boys' I could find, if I knew he was coming." I knew this man meant what he said, for the men of the regiment knew Colonel Trowbridge first of all the other officers. He was with them on St. Simon and at Camp Saxton. I remember when the company was being formed, we wished Captain C. T. was our captain, because most of the men in Co. E were the men he brought with him from St. Simon, and they were attached to him. He was always jolly and pleasing with all. I remember, when going into Savannah in 1865, he said that he had been there before the war, and told me many things I did not know about the river. Although this was my home, I had never been on it before. No officer in the army was more beloved than our late lieutenant-colonel, C. T. Trowbridge.

C. T. Trowbridge
Lieut. Col. 33d U.S.C.T.

*[Copy of General Orders.]*
"GENERAL ORDERS.

"Headquarters 33d U.S.C.T.,
"Late 1st So. Carolina Volunteers,
"Morris Island, S. C., Feb. 9, 1866.

*"General Order,*
*"No. 1.*

"COMRADES: The hour is at hand when we must separate forever, and nothing can take from us the pride we feel, when we look upon the history of the 'First South Carolina Volunteers,' the first black regiment that ever bore arms in defense of freedom on the continent of America.

"On the 9th day of May, 1862, at which time there were nearly four millions of your race in bondage, sanctioned by the laws of the land and protected by our flag,—on that day, in the face of the floods of prejudice that well-nigh deluged every avenue to manhood and true liberty, you came forth to do battle for your country and kindred.

"For long and weary months, without pay or even the privilege of being recognized as soldiers, you labored on, only to be disbanded[1] and sent to your homes without even a hope of reward, and when our country, necessitated by the deadly struggle with armed traitors, finally granted you the opportunity again to come forth in defense of the nation's life, the alacrity with which you responded to the call[1] gave abundant evidence of your readiness to strike a manly blow for the liberty of your race.[2] And from that little band of hopeful, trusting, and brave men who gathered at Camp Saxton, on Port Royal Island, in the fall of '62, amidst the terrible prejudices that surrounded us, has grown an army of a hundred and forty thousand black soldiers, whose valor and heroism has won for your race a name which will live as long as the undying pages of history shall endure; and by whose efforts, united with those of the white man, armed rebellion has been conquered, the millions of bondsmen have been emancipated, and the fundamental law of the land has been so altered as to remove forever the possibility of human slavery being established within the borders of redeemed America. The flag of our fathers, restored to its rightful significance, now floats over every foot of our territory, from Maine to California, and beholds only free men! The prejudices which formerly existed against you are well-nigh rooted out.[3]

"Soldiers, you have done your duty and acquitted yourselves like men who, actuated by such ennobling motives, could not fail; and as the result of your fidelity and obedience you have won your freedom, and oh, how great the reward! It seems fitting to me that the last hours of our existence as a regiment should be passed amidst the unmarked graves of your comrades, at Fort Wagner. Near you rest the bones of Colonel Shaw, buried by an enemy's hand in the same grave with his black soldiers who fell at his side; where in the future your children's children will come on pilgrimages to do homage to the ashes of those who fell in this glorious struggle.

"The flag which was presented to us by the Rev. George B. Cheever and his congregation, of New York City, on the 1st of January, 1863,—the day when Lincoln's immortal proclamation of freedom was given to the world,—and which you have done so nobly through the war, is now to be rolled up forever and deposited in our nation's capital. And while there it shall rest, with the battles in which you have participated inscribed upon its folds, it will be a source of pride to us all to remember that it has never been disgraced by a cowardly faltering in the hour of danger, or polluted by a traitor's touch.

"Now that you are to lay aside your arms, I adjure you, by the associations and history of the past, and the love you bear for your liberties, to harbor no feelings of hatred toward your former masters, but to seek in the paths of honesty, virtue, sobriety, and industry, and by a willing obedience to the laws of the land, to grow up to the full stature of American citizens. The church, the school-house, and the right forever to be free are now secured to you, and every prospect before you is full of hope and encouragement. The nation guarantees to you full protection and justice, and will require from you in return that respect for the laws and orderly deportment which will prove to every one your right to all the privileges of freemen. To the officers of the regiment I would say, your toils are ended, your mission is fulfilled, and we separate forever. The fidelity, patience, and patriotism with which you have discharged your duties to your men and to your country entitle you to a far higher tribute than any words of thankfulness which I can give you from the bottom of my heart. You will find your reward in the proud conviction that the cause for which you have battled so nobly has been crowned with abundant success.

"Officers and soldiers of the 33d U. S. Colored Troops, once the First So. Carolina Volunteers, I bid you all farewell![4]

"By order of

"LT. COLONEL C. T. TROWBRIDGE,
"*Commanding regiment.*


"E. W. HYDE,
"1st Lieut. 33d U.S.C.T. and acting adjutant."


I have one of the original copies of these orders still in my possession.


My dear friends! do we understand the meaning of war? Do we know or think of that war of '61? No, we do not, only those brave soldiers, and those who had occasion to be in it, can realize what it was. I can and shall never forget that terrible war until my eyes close in death. The scenes are just as fresh in my mind to-day as in '61. I see now each scene,—the roll-call, the drum tap, "lights out," the call at night when there was danger from the enemy, the double force of pickets, the cold and rain. How anxious I would be, not knowing what would happen before morning! Many times I would dress, not sure but all would be captured. Other times I would stand at my tent door and try to see what was going on, because night was the time the rebels would try to get into our lines and capture some of the boys. It was mostly at night that our men went out for their scouts, and often had a hand to hand fight with the rebels, and although our men came out sometimes with a few killed or wounded, none of them ever were captured.

We do not, as the black race, properly appreciate the old veterans, white or black, as we ought to. I know what they went through, especially those black men, for the Confederates had no mercy on them; neither did they show any toward the white Union soldiers. I have seen the terrors of that war. I was the wife of one of those men who did not get a penny for eighteen months for their services, only their rations and clothing.

I cannot praise General David Hunter too highly, for he was the first man to arm the black man, in the beginning of 1862.[5] He had a hard struggle to hold all the Southern division, with so few men, so he applied to Congress; but the answer to him was, "Do not bother us," which was very discouraging. As the general needed more men to protect the islands and do garrison duty, he organized two companies.

I look around now and see the comforts that our younger generation enjoy,[6] and think of the blood that was shed to make these comforts possible for them, and see how little some of them appreciate the old soldiers. My heart burns within me, at this want of appreciation. There are only a few of them left now, so let us all, as the ranks close, take a deeper interest also, and remember that it was through the efforts of these veterans that they and we older ones enjoy our liberty today.

Notes on chapter *X*.

[1] Colonel Trowbridge refers to the disbanding of Hunter's regiment and its subsequent reinstatement as the enlarged First South Carolina Volunteers, by General Saxton. Douglas Cornish writes: "In justice to Hunter and Trowbridge and in recognition of the patient fortitude and sacrifice of their red-trousered men, the 1st South Carolina deserves to be called the first American Negro regiment. Its survival through the summer and fall of 1862 contributed immeasurably to the ultimate success of the movement to permit the American Negro to fight for his own freedom." (Cornish, pp. 92–93)

[2] Although many of them were glad to serve, the freedman did not always come voluntarily into the Army's ranks. There is evidence that many recruiters, both black and white, forced the liberated slaves into the Army, even at gunpoint, in order to fill the ranks as fast as possible. General Saxton, under whose orders the army was raised, strongly opposed these tactics, but he was not always able to control his subordinates' wholesale recruiting activities.

[3] The optimism of the antislavery movement was such that Union victory meant the end of reduced status for the Negro to those who, like Trowbridge, had little contact with the more prejudiced mass of Americans. Most abolitionists and freedmen shared this hopefulness—it was to them an antislavery victory. (The abolitionists' idealism is further exhibited in Col. Trowbridge's remarks in the second paragraph on page 49.) This optimism carried over into Reconstruction, but was short-lived. Even though it spelled the end of the institution of slavery, reunification of the country did not end widespread bigotry.

[4] Many South Carolinians who served in the regiment continued to serve their country in various ways. Some remained in the army and were sent to defend the country's western frontiers. Others participated as elected and appointed officials in Reconstruction politics.

[5] General Hunter raised those first troops illegally, however, and recruiting practices in the 1862 effort were sufficiently harsh to turn many freedmen against army life permanently.

[6] Despite the prejudice and bigotry aimed at blacks after the war, the contrast between freedom and slavery was very marked to Mrs. Taylor, a former Georgia slave who was residing in Massachusetts as she wrote these words.

# XI
## *AFTER THE WAR*

In 1866, the steamers which ran from Savannah to Darien would not take colored people unless they stayed in a certain part of the boat, away from the white people;[1] so some of the colored citizens and ex-soldiers decided to form a syndicate and buy a steamer of their own. They finally bought a large one of a New York company. It arrived in fine shape, apparently, and made its first trip to Darien. The next trip was to Beaufort. I went on this trip, as the pilot, James Cook, was a friend of my family, and I thought I would enjoy the trip; and I did, getting back in safety. The next trip was to go to Florida, but it never reached there, for on the way down the boat ran upon St. John bar and went entirely to pieces. They found out afterward that they had been swindled, as the boat was a condemned one, and the company took advantage of them; and as they carried no insurance on the boat they lost all the money they had invested in it. The best people of the city expressed great sympathy for them in their loss, as it promised to prove a great investment at first.

At the close of the war, my husband and I returned to Savannah, a number of the comrades returning at the same time. A new life was before us now, all the old life left behind. After getting settled, I opened a school at my home on South Broad Street, now called Oglethorpe Avenue, as there was not any public school for negro children. I had twenty children at my school, and received one dollar a month for each pupil. I also had a few older ones who came at night. There were several other private schools[2] besides mine. Mrs. Lucinda Jackson had one on the same street I lived on.

I taught almost a year, when the Beach Institute[3] opened, which took a number of my scholars, as this was a free school. On September 16, 1866, my husband, Sergeant King, died, leaving me soon to welcome a little stranger alone. He was a boss carpenter, but being just mustered out of the army, and the prejudice against his race being still too strong to insure him much work at his trade,[4] he took contracts for unloading vessels, and hired a number of men to assist him. He was much respected by the citizens, and was a general favorite with his associates.

In December, 1866, I was obliged to give up

Susie King Taylor's Schoolhouse in Savannah

teaching, but in April, 1867, I opened a school in Liberty County, Georgia, and taught there one year; but country life did not agree with me, so I returned to the city, and Mrs. Susie Carrier took charge of my school.

On my return to Savannah, I found that the free school had taken all my former pupils, so I opened a night school, where I taught a number of adults. This, together with other things I could get to do and the assistance of my brother-in-law, supported me. I taught this school until the fall of 1868, when a free night school opened at the Beach Institute, and again my scholars left me to attend this free school. So I had to close my school. I put my baby with my mother and entered in the employ of a family, where I lived quite a while, but had to leave, as the work was too hard.

In 1872 I put in a claim for my husband's bounty and received one hundred dollars, some of which I put in the Freedmen's Savings Bank.[5] In the fall of 1872 I went to work for a very wealthy lady, Mrs. Charles Green, as laundress. In the spring of 1873, Mr. and Mrs. Green came North to Rye Beach for the summer, and as their cook did not care to go so far from home, I went with them in her place.[6] While there, I won a prize for excellent cooking at a fair which the ladies who were summering there had held to raise funds to build an Episcopal Church, and Mrs. Green was one of the energetic workers to make this fair a success;

and it was a success in every respect and a tidy sum was netted.

I returned South with Mrs. Green, and soon after, she went to Europe. I returned to Boston again in 1874, through the kindness of Mrs. Barnard, a daughter of ex-Mayor Otis of Boston. She was accompanied by her husband, Mr. James Barnard (who was an agent for the line of steamers), her six children, the nurse, and myself. We left Savannah on the steamship Seminole, under Captain Matthews, and when we had passed Hatteras some distance, she broke her shaft. The captain had the sails hoisted and we drifted along, there being a stiff breeze, which was greatly in our favor. Captain Matthews said the nearest point he could make was Cape Henry Light. About noon, Mr. Barnard spied the light and told the captain if he would give him a boat and some of the crew, he would row to the light for help. This was done, the boat was manned and they put off. They made the light, then they made for Norfolk, which was eight miles from the light, and did not reach the city until eight o'clock that night.

Next morning he returned with a tug, to tow us into Norfolk for repairs; but the tug was too small to move the steamer, so it went back for more help, but before it returned, a Norfolk steamer, on its way to Boston, stopped to see what was the matter with our steamer. Mr. Barnard remained on the steamer, and Mrs.

Barnard deciding to remain with him, I went aboard this other steamer with the rest of the passengers. We left them at anchor, waiting for the tugs to return.

This accident brought back very vividly the time previous to this, when I was in that other wreck in 1864, and I wondered if they would reach port safe, for it is a terrible thing to be cast away; but on arriving in Boston, about two days later, I was delighted to hear of the arrival of their steamer at T Wharf, with all on board safe.

Soon after I got to Boston, I entered the service of Mr. Thomas Smith's family, on Walnut Avenue, Boston Highlands, where I remained until the death of Mrs. Smith. I next lived with Mrs. Gorham Gray, Beacon Street, where I remained until I was married, in 1879, to Russell L. Taylor.

In 1880 I had another experience in steamer accidents. Mr. Taylor and I started for New York on the steamer Stonington. We were in bed when, sometime in the night, the Narragansett collided with our boat. I was awakened by the crash. I was in the ladies' cabin. There were about thirty-five or forty others in the cabin. I sprang out of my berth, dressed as quickly as I could, and tried to reach the deck, but we found the cabin door locked, and two men stood outside and would not let us out. About twenty minutes after, they opened the doors and we went up on deck, and a terrible scene was before us. The Narragansett was on fire, in a bright blaze; the water was lighted as far as one could see, the passengers shrieking, groaning, running about, leaping into the water, panic-stricken. A steamer came to our assistance; they put the life-rafts off and saved a great many from the burning steamer, and picked a number up from the water. A colored man saved his wife and child by giving each a chair and having them jump overboard. These chairs kept them afloat until they were taken aboard by the life-raft. The steamer was burned to the water's edge. The passengers on board our steamer were transferred to another one and got to New York at 9.30 the next morning. A number of lives were lost in this accident, and the bow of the Stonington was badly damaged. I was thankful for my escape, for I had been in two similar experiences and got off safely, and I have come to the conclusion I shall never have a watery grave.

Notes on chapter *XI*.

[1] This is an instance of the black codes, or anti-Negro laws, passed by southern states at the end of the war. The black codes were the South's response to the Emancipation Proclamation. Primarily, the codes aimed at keeping blacks in low-status agricultural work and limiting their civil rights. But the codes imposed other limitations on black people which made equality an impossible ideal.

[2] Education was one of the most prized aspects of freedom. Horace Mann Bond wrote, "No mass movement has been more in the American tradition than the urge which drove Negroes toward education soon after the Civil War."

[3] The Freedmen's Bureau built this school on lands purchased by the American Missionary Association. Funds were furnished by Alfred E. Beach, editor of the *Scientific American*. Beach Institute was dedicated on January 1, 1868.

[4] Another of the black codes forbade freedmen to pursue free labor—they were forced to work under contract with an employer, preferably in farm work. To enforce this, unemployed blacks were treated harshly under the codes' unfair vagrancy laws. This successfully drove many blacks out of the cities.

[5] A little state and local aid had been made available to dependents of some Northern black soldiers, but Federal pensions did not become available until July, 1864 for widows and orphans—on the condition that they were free. The one hundred dollar bounty automatically given since the war's third month to all white soldiers upon their mustering in the Union army also became available to black soldiers around the same time along with pay retroactive to January 1, 1864, provided the soldiers had been free when the war began. This provision therefore excluded the bulk of the Southern black soldiers. Finally in March, 1865, the Southern black soldiers were paid in full, from the date of their enlistment. Ironically, as early as October, 1863, slaveowners whose property had become Union soldiers were entitled to receive three hundred dollars compensation for each such slave.

[6] Rye Beach is a New Hampshire ocean resort, about fifty miles north of Boston.

# XII

# THE WOMEN'S RELIEF CORPS

ALL this time my interest in the boys in blue had not abated. I was still loyal and true, whether they were black or white. My hands have never left undone anything they could do toward their aid and comfort in the twilight of their lives. In 1886 I helped to organize Corps 67, Women's Relief Corps, auxiliary to the G. A. R., and it is a very flourishing corps to-day.[1] I have been Guard, Secretary, Treasurer for three years, and in 1893 I was made President of this corps, Mrs. Emily Clark being Department President this year. In 1896, in response to an order sent out by the Department W. R. C. to take a census to secure a complete roster of the Union Veterans of the War of the Rebellion now residing in Massachusetts, I was allotted the West End district, which (with the assistance of Mrs. Lizzie L. Johnson, a member of Corps 67, and widow of a soldier of the 54th Mass. Volunteers) I canvassed with splendid success, and found a great many comrades who were not attached to any post in the city or State.

In 1898 the Department of Mass. W. R. C. gave a grand fair at Music Hall. I made a large quilt of red, white, and blue ribbon that made quite a sensation. The quilt was voted for and was awarded to the Department President, Mrs. E. L. W. Waterman, of Boston.

Notes on chapter *XII*.

[1] The Grand Army of the Republic was the Union veterans' organization. Mostly Republican, this group was significant politically, in addition to its work for veterans' causes.

# XIII
## THOUGHTS ON PRESENT CONDITIONS

LIVING here in Boston where the black man
is given equal justice, I must say a word on the
general treatment of my race, both in the North
and South, in this twentieth century. I wonder
if our white fellow men realize the true sense
or meaning of brotherhood? For two hundred
years[1] we had toiled for them; the war of 1861
came and was ended, and we thought our race
was forever free from bondage, and that the
two races could live in unity with each other,
but when we read almost every day of what is
being done to my race by some whites in the
South, I sometimes ask, "Was the war in vain?
Has it brought freedom, in the full sense of the
word, or has it not made our condition more
hopeless?"

In this "land of the free" we are burned,
tortured, and denied a fair trial, murdered for
any imaginary wrong conceived in the brain of

the negro-hating white man.[2] There is no re-
dress for us from a government which promised to protect all under its flag. It seems a
mystery to me. They say, "One flag, one nation, one country indivisible." Is this true? Can
we say this truthfully, when one race is allowed
to burn, hang, and inflict the most horrible
torture weekly, monthly, on another? No, we
cannot sing, "My country 't is of thee, Sweet
land of Liberty"! It is hollow mockery. The
Southland laws are all on the side of the white,
and they do just as they like to the negro,
whether in the right or not.[3]

I do not uphold my race when they do
wrong. They ought to be punished, but the
innocent are made to suffer as well as the
guilty, and I hope the time will hasten when it
will be stopped forever. Let us remember God
says, "He that sheds blood, his blood shall be
required again." I may not live to see it, but the
time is approaching when the South will again
have cause to repent for the blood it has shed
of innocent black men, for their blood cries out
for vengeance. For the South still cherishes a
hatred toward the blacks, although there are
some true Southern gentlemen left who abhor
the stigma brought upon them, and feel it very
keenly, and I hope the day is not far distant
when the two races will reside in peace in the
Southland, and we will sing with sincere and
truthful hearts, "My country, 't is of thee,
Sweet land of Liberty, of thee I sing."

I have been in many States and cities, and in each I have looked for liberty and justice, equal for the black as for the white; but it was not until I was within the borders of New England, and reached old Massachusetts, that I found it. Here is found liberty in the full sense of the word, liberty for the stranger within her gates, irrespective of race or creed, liberty and justice for all.

We have before us still another problem to solve. With the close of the Spanish war, and on the entrance of the Americans into Cuba, the same conditions confront us as the war of 1861 left. The Cubans are free, but it is a limited freedom, for prejudice, deep-rooted, has been brought to them and a separation made between the white and black Cubans, a thing that had never existed between them before; but to-day there is the same intense hatred toward the negro in Cuba that there is in some parts of this country.

I helped to furnish and pack boxes to be sent to the soldiers and hospitals during the first part of the Spanish war; there were black soldiers there too. At the battle of San Juan Hill, they were in the front, just as brave, loyal, and true as those other black men who fought for freedom and the right, and yet their bravery and faithfulness were reluctantly acknowledged, and praise grudgingly given. All we ask for is "equal justice," the same that is accorded to all other races who come to this country, of their free will (not forced to, as we were), and are allowed to enjoy every privilege, unrestricted, while we are denied what is rightfully our own in a country which the labor of our forefathers helped to make what it is.

One thing I have noticed among my people in the South: they have accumulated a large amount of real estate, far surpassing the colored owners in the North, who seem to let their opportunity slip by them.[4] Nearly all of Brownsville (a suburb of Savannah) is owned by colored people, and so it is in a great many other places throughout the State, and all that is needed is the protection of the law as citizens.

In 1867, soon after the death of my father, who had served on a gunboat during the war, my mother opened a grocery store, where she kept general merchandise always on hand. These she traded for cash or would exchange for crops of cotton, corn, or rice, which she would ship once a month, to F. Lloyd & Co., or Johnson & Jackson, in Savannah. These were colored merchants, doing business on Bay Street in that city. Mother bought her first property, which contained ten acres. She next purchased fifty acres of land. Then she had a chance to get a place with seven hundred acres of land, and she bought this.

In 1870, Colonel Hamilton and Major Devendorft, of Oswego, N. Y., came to the town and bought up a tract of land at a place called Doctortown, and started a mill. Mrs. Devendorft heard of my mother and went to see her, and persuaded her to come to live with her, assuring her she would be as one of the family. Mother went with her, but after a few months she went to Doctortown, where she has been since, and now owns the largest settlement there. All trains going to Florida pass her place, just across the Altamaha River. She is well known by both white and black; the people are fond of her, and will not allow any one to harm her.

Mr. Devendorft sold out his place in 1880 and went back to New York, where later he died.

I read an article, which said the ex-Confederate Daughters[5] had sent a petition to the managers of the local theatres in Tennessee to prohibit the performance of "Uncle Tom's Cabin," claiming it was exaggerated (that is, the treatment of the slaves), and would have a very bad effect on the children who might see the drama. I paused and thought back a few years of the heart-rending scenes I have witnessed; I have seen many times, when I was a mere girl, thirty or forty men, handcuffed, and as many women and children, come every first Tuesday of each month from Mr. Wiley's trade office to the auction blocks, one of them being situated on Drayton Street and Court Lane, the other on Bryant Street, near the Pulaski House.

The route was down our principal street, Bull Street, to the court-house, which was only a block from where I resided.

All people in those days got all their water from the city pumps, which stood about a block apart throughout the city. The one we used to get water from was opposite the court-house, on Bull Street. I remember, as if it were yesterday, seeing droves of negroes going to be sold, and I often went to look at them, and I could hear the auctioneer very plainly from my house, auctioning these poor people off.

Do these Confederate Daughters ever send petitions to prohibit the atrocious lynchings and wholesale murdering and torture of the negro? Do you ever hear of them fearing this would have a bad effect on the children?[6] Which of these two, the drama or the present state of affairs, makes a degrading impression upon the minds of our young generation! In my opinion it is not "Uncle Tom's Cabin," but it should be the one that has caused the world to cry "Shame!" It does not seem as if our land is yet civilized. It is like times long past, when rulers and high officers had to flee for their lives, and the negro has been dealt with in the same way since the war by those he lived with and toiled for two hundred years or more. I do not condemn all the Caucasian race because the negro is badly treated by a few of the race. No! for had it not been for the true whites, assisted by God and the prayers of our fore-fathers, I should not be here to-day.

There are still good friends to the negro. Why, there are still thousands that have not bowed to Baal.[7] So it is with us. Man thinks two hundred years is a long time, and it is too; but it is only as a week to God, and in his own time—I know I shall not live to see the day, but it will come—the South will be like the North, and when it comes it will be prized higher than we prize the North to-day. God is just; when he created man he made him in his image, and never intended one should misuse the other. All men are born free and equal in his sight.

I am pleased to know at this writing that the officers and comrades of my regiment stand ready to render me assistance whenever required. It seems like "bread cast upon the water," and it has returned after many days, when it is most needed. I have received letters from some of the comrades, since we parted in 1866, with expressions of gratitude and thanks to me for teaching them their first letters. One of them, Peter Waggall, is a minister in Jacksonville, Fla. Another is in the government service at Washington, D.C. Others are in Darien and Savannah, Ga., and all are doing well.

There are many people who do not know what some of the colored women did during the war. There were hundreds of them who assisted the Union soldiers by hiding them and helping them to escape.[8] Many were punished for taking food to the prison stockades for the prisoners. When I went into Savannah, in 1865, I was told of one of these stockades which was in the suburbs of the city, and they said it was an awful place. The Union soldiers were in it, worse than pigs, without any shelter from sun or storm, and the colored women would take food there at night and pass it to them, through the holes in the fence. The soldiers were starving, and these women did all they could toward relieving those men, although they knew the penalty, should they be caught giving them aid. Others assisted in various ways the Union army. These things should be kept in history before the people. There has never been a greater war in the United States than the one of 1861, where so many lives were lost,—not men alone but noble women as well.[9]

Let us not forget that terrible war, or our brave soldiers who were thrown into Andersonville and Libby prisons, the awful agony they went through, and the most brutal treatment they received in those loathsome dens, the worst ever given human beings; and if the white soldiers were subjected to such treatment, what must have been the horrors inflicted on the negro soldiers in their prison pens? Can we forget these cruelties? No, though we try to forgive and say, "No North, no South," and hope to see it in reality before the last comrade passes away.

Notes on chapter *XIII.*

[1] The first Africans were brought to this country in 1619, nearly three hundred years before Mrs. Taylor wrote her reminiscences.

[2] Tuskeegee Institute reported that eighty-five Negroes were lynched in 1902, the year this book was first published. There were, of course, countless unknown and unreported instances of other forms of physical persecution, in both the South and the North. The prejudice to which Mrs. Taylor refers here did not abate in her lifetime, but reached a peak in the 1920s with a revival of the Ku Klux Klan.

[3] The black codes were rescinded by the fairer Reconstruction laws in Southern states, but the post-Reconstruction period ("Redemption," as Southerners called it) saw a new set of prejudicial laws imposed on blacks. These "Jim Crow" laws were also found to a lesser degree in the North.

[4] The Southern agricultural economy meant that survival was equated with landholding. Freedmen had been prevented from acquiring land for many years in the South—by law and by tradition. Since the only skill many freedmen possessed was farming, this meant they could never attain self-sufficiency, because farm labor wages never rose above mere subsistence level. Naturally, when opportunities to buy land were made available to blacks, even in urban areas, they were quickly acted upon.

[5] The United Daughters of the Confederacy, an organization which is still active, was roughly the Southern counterpart to the Women's Relief Corps of the G. A. R.

[6] The psychological damage which lynching inflicted on children, black *and* white, was a theme used in the NAACP's effective crusades against lynching in the 1910s and 1920s.

[7] This is a biblical allusion to idolatry, meaning "turned away from God."

[8] James McPherson writes of these secret helpers: "Throughout the war Southern Negroes rendered valuable assistance to Northern soldiers who had escaped from Confederate prisons and were trying to find their way back to Union lines. . . . The prison literature of the Civil War is full of stories about slaves who helped escaping Yankee soldiers." (McPherson, p. 150)

[9] Despite the wars in which the United States has taken part since Mrs. Taylor wrote these lines, her statement is as true now as when she wrote it. The Civil War claimed more American lives (498,443) than any other war.

# XIV
## A VISIT TO LOUISIANA

THE inevitable always happens. On February 3, 1898, I was called to Shreveport, La., to the bedside of my son, who was very ill. He was traveling with Nickens and Company, with "The Lion's Bride," when he fell ill, and had been ill two weeks when they sent to me. I tried to have him brought home to Boston, but they could not send him, as he was not able to sit and ride this long distance; so on the sixth of February I left Boston to go to him. I reached Cincinnati on the eighth, where I took the train for the south. I asked a white man standing near (before I got my train) what car I should take. "Take that one," he said, pointing to one. "But that is a smoking car!" "Well," he replied, "that is the car for colored people." I went to this car, and on entering it all my courage failed me. I have ridden in many coaches, but I was never in such as these. I wanted to return home again, but when I thought of my sick boy I said, "Well, others ride in these cars and I must do likewise," and tried to be resigned, for I wanted to reach my boy, as I did not know whether I should find him alive. I arrived in Chattanooga at eight o'clock in the evening, where the porter took my baggage to the train which was to leave for Marion, Miss. Soon after I was seated, just before the train pulled out, two tall men with slouch hats on walked through the car, and on through the train. Finally they came back to our car and stopping at my seat said, "Where are those men who were with you?" I did not know to whom they were speaking, as there was another woman in the car, so I made no reply. Again they asked me, standing directly in front of my seat, "Where are those men who came in with you?" "Are you speaking of me?" I said. "Yes!" they said. "I have not seen any men," I replied. They looked at me a moment, and one of them asked where I was from. I told him Boston; he hesitated a minute and walked out of our car to the other car.

When the conductor came around I told him what these men had said, and asked him if they allowed persons to enter the car and insult passengers. He only smiled. Later, when the porter came in, I mentioned it to him. He said, "Lady, I see you do not belong here; where are you from?" I told him. He said, "I have often heard of Massachusetts.[1] I want to see that place." "Yes!" I said, "you can ride there on the cars, and no person would be allowed to speak to you as those men did to me." He explained that those men were constables, who were in search of a man who had eloped with another man's wife. "That is the way they do here. Each morning you can hear of some negro being lynched"; and on seeing my surprise, he said, "Oh, that is nothing; it is done all the time. We have no rights here. I have been on this road for fifteen years and have seen some terrible things." He wanted to know what I was doing down there, and I told him it was only the illness of my son that brought me there.

I was a little surprised at the way the poor whites were made to ride on this road.[2] They put them all together by themselves in a car, between the colored people's coach and the first-class coach, and it looked like the "Laborers' car" used in Boston to carry the different day laborers to and from their work.

I got to Marion, Miss., at two o'clock in the morning, arrived at Vicksburg at noon, and at Shreveport about eight o'clock in the evening, and found my son just recovering from a severe hemorrhage. He was very anxious to come home, and I tried to secure a berth for him on a sleeper, but they would not sell me one, and he was not strong enough to travel otherwise. If I could only have gotten him to Cincinnati, I might have brought him home, but as I could not I was forced to let him remain where he was. It seemed very hard, when his father fought to protect the Union and our flag, and yet this boy was denied, under this same flag, a berth to carry him home to die, because he was a negro.

Shreveport is a little town, made up largely of Jews and Germans and a few Southerners, the negroes being in the majority. Its sidewalks are sand except on the main street. Almost all the stores are kept either by the Jews or Germans. They know a stranger in a minute, as the town is small and the citizens know each other; if not personally, their faces are familiar.

I went into a jewelry store one day to have a crystal put in my watch, and the attendant remarked, "You are a stranger." I asked him how he knew that. He said he had watched me for a week or so. I told him yes, I was a stranger and from Boston. "Oh! I have heard of Boston," he said. "You will not find this place like it is there. How do you like this town?" "Not very well," I replied.

I found that the people who lived in Massachusetts and were settled in Shreveport were very cordial to me and glad to see me. There was a man murdered in cold blood for nothing. He was a colored man and a "porter" in a store in this town. A clerk had left his umbrella at home. It had begun to rain when he started for home, and on looking for the umbrella he could not, of course, find it. He asked the porter if he had seen it. He said no, he had not.

"You answer very saucy," said the clerk, and drawing his revolver, he shot the colored man dead. He was taken up the street to an office where he was placed under one thousand dollars bond for his appearance and released, and that was the end of the case. I was surprised at this, but I was told by several white and colored persons that this was a common occurrence, and the persons were never punished if they were white, but no mercy was shown to negroes.

I met several comrades, white and colored, there, and noticed that the colored comrades did not wear their buttons.[3] I asked one of them why this was, and was told, should they wear it, they could not get work.[4] Still some would wear their buttons in spite of the feeling against it. I met a newsman from New York on the train. He was a veteran, and said that Sherman ought to come back and go into that part of the country.

Shreveport is a horrid place when it rains. The earth is red and sticks to your shoes, and it is impossible to keep rubbers on, for the mud pulls them off. Going across the Mississippi River, I was amazed to see how the houses were built, so close to the shore, or else on low land; and when the river rises, it flows into these houses and must make it very disagreeable and unhealthy for the inmates.

After the death of my son, while on my way back to Boston, I came to Clarksdale, one of the stations on the road from Vicksburg. In this town a Mr. Hancock, of New York, had a large cotton plantation, and the Chinese intermarry with the blacks.

At Clarksdale, I saw a man hanged. It was a terrible sight, and I felt alarmed for my own safety down there. When I reached Memphis I found conditions of travel much better. The people were mostly Western and Northern here; the cars were nice, but separate for colored persons until we reached the Ohio River, when the door was opened and the porter passed through, saying, "The Ohio River! change to the other car." I thought, "What does he mean? We have been riding all this distance in separate cars, and now we are all to sit together." It certainly seemed a peculiar arrangement. Why not let the negroes, if their appearance and respectability warrant it, be allowed to ride as they do in the North, East, or West?

There are others besides the blacks, in the South and North, that should be put in separate cars while traveling, just as they put my race. Many black people in the South do not wish to be thrown into a car because all are colored, as there are many of their race very objectionable to them, being of an entirely different class; but they have to adapt themselves to the circumstances and ride with them, because they are all negroes. There is no such division with the whites. Except in one place I saw, the workingman and the millionaire ride in the same coaches together. Why not allow the respectable, law-abiding classes of the blacks the same privilege? We hope for better conditions in the future, and feel sure they will come in time, surely if slowly.

While in Shreveport, I visited ex-Senator Harper's house. He is a colored man and owns a large business block, besides a fine residence on Cado Street and several good building lots. Another family, the Pages, living on the same street, were quite wealthy, and a large number of colored families owned their homes, and were industrious, refined people; and if they were only allowed justice, the South would be the only place for our people to live.

We are similar to the children of Israel,[5] who, after many weary years in bondage, were led into that land of promise, there to thrive and be forever free from persecution; and I don't despair, for the Book which is our guide through life declares, "Ethiopia shall stretch forth her hand."

What a wonderful revolution! In 1861 the Southern papers were full of advertisements for "slaves," but now, despite all the hindrances and "race problems," my people are striving to attain the full standard of all other races born free in the sight of God, and in a number of instances have succeeded. Justice we ask,—to be citizens of these United States, where so many of our people have shed their blood with their white comrades, that the stars and stripes should never be polluted.

### Notes on chapter *XIV*.

[1] Although in fact it was far from being truly democratic, Massachusetts was probably the most forward-looking state. In many ways the state was held in near reverence by Negroes; it was a kind of promised land of equality among all the states, having had a long history of liberalism and abolitionism. Massachusetts produced many statesmen and writers who spoke out boldly and effectively for equality.

[2] At the turn of the century economic and social discrimination of all sorts was generally accepted. Even Mrs. Taylor does not find class discrimination inconsistent with her own ideas of equality and democracy. (see p. 74)

[3] The buttons referred to were veterans' insignia.

[4] There was still much resentment against both the Union cause and the Afro-Americans who had fought for their freedom that Southerners were even harsher in their attitudes toward these Union veterans than toward blacks in general.

[5] This reference is to the ancient Jews, held in slavery and bondage and persecuted by the Egyptians until Moses led them out, toward the "promised land," then called Ethiopia.

# SELECT BIBLIOGRAPHY OF SOURCES USED

*American Missionary,* Vol. XIII, No. 4, Memphis, American Missionary Association Archives, LeMoyne College, April, 1869.

Bennett, Lerone, Jr., *Black Power USA: The Human Side of Reconstruction 1867–1877,* (Chicago, 1967).

———. *Before the Mayflower,* (Chicago, 1962).

Billington, Ray Allen (ed. and introduction) *Journal of Charlotte Forten,* (New York, 1953).

Blasingame, John (ed). *Slave Testimony: Two Centuries of Letters, Speeches, Interviews, and Autobiographies,* (Baton Rouge, 1977).

Bond, Horace Mann, *The Education of the Negro in the American Social Order,* (New York, 1966).

Cornish, Dudley Taylor, *The Sable Arm,* (New York, 1966).

Cutler, Andrews J., *The South Reports The Civil War* (Princeton, 1970).

Gutman, Herbert, *The Black Family in Slavery and Freedom 1750–1925,* (New York, 1976).

Guzman, Jessie P., and Jones, Lewis W., (eds.), *1952 Negro Year Book,* (New York, 1952).

Higginson, Thomas Wentworth, *Army Life in a Black Regiment,* (Boston, 1870).

Holmgren, Virginia C., *Hilton Head, A Sea Island Chronicle,* (Hilton Head, South Carolina, 1959).

Huggins, Nathan I., *Black Odyssey: The Afro-American Ordeal in Slavery,* (New York, 1977).

Litwack, Leon F., *Been in the Storm so Long: The Emergence of Black Freedom in the South,* (New York, 1979).

———, *North of Slavery,* (Chicago, 1961).

Loewenberg, Bert J., & Bogin, Ruth, (eds.), *Black Women in Nineteenth Century American Life* (University Park, Pennsylvania, 1976).

MacPherson, James, *The Negro's Civil War*, (New York, 1965).

Meier, August & Rudwick, Elliott M., *From Plantation to Ghetto*, (New York, 1966).

Metcalf, Clyde H., *A History of the United States Marines*, (New York, 1939).

Oubré, Claude, *Forty Acres and a Mule*, (Baton Rouge, 1977).

Quarles, Benjamin, *The Negro in the Civil War*, (New York, 1968).

Randall, J. G., & Donald, David, *The Divided Union*, (Boston, 1961).

Rose, Willie Lee, *Rehearsal for Reconstruction: The Port Royal Experiment*, (Baltimore, 1962).

Simkin, Francis Butler, *A History of the South*, (New York, 1956).

Stampp, Kenneth M., *The Peculiar Institution: Slavery in the Ante-Bellum South*, (New York, 1956).

Stillman, Richard J., II, *Integration of the Negro in the U.S. Armed Forces*, (New York, 1968).

Vanstory, Burnette, *Georgia's Land of the Golden Isles*. (Athens, Georgia, 1956).

Wade, Richard C., *Slavery in the Cities: The South 1820–1860*, (New York, 1964).

Weyl, Nathaniel, *The Negro in American Civilization*, (Washington, D. C., 1960).

Williamson, Joel, *After Slavery: The Negro in South Carolina During Reconstruction, 1861–1877*, (Chapel Hill, 1965).

Wilson, Theodore B., *The Black Codes of the South*, (Montgomery, Alabama, 1965).

Woodward, C. Vann, *The Strange Career of Jim Crow*, (New York, 1957).

# ABOUT THE EDITORS

WILLIE LEE ROSE is the author of numerous prize-winning books, including *Rehearsal for Reconstruction* (1964 and 1976), *Slavery and Freedom* (with William W. Freehling, 1982), and *A Documentary History of Slavery in North America* (1976). She has published many articles in the *New York Review of Books* and in scholarly journals. After her tenure as Commonwealth Professor of American History at the University of Virginia and a series of distinguished appointments, Professor Rose was the first woman to be appointed Harmsworth Professor at Oxford University (1977-78). In 1973 she began teaching at Johns Hopkins University, where she is now professor emeritus. Among her most recent awards is the 1990 Distinguished Service Award of the Organization of American Historians.

PATRICIA W. ROMERO is the author of *E. Sylvia Pankhurst: Portrait of a Radical* (1988) and the editor of several books including *Women's Voices on Africa* (1992), Emily Ruete's *Memoirs of an Arabian Princess from Zanzibar* (1990), *Life Histories of African Women* (1989), *In Black America* (1969), and *I, Too, Am America* (1968). She is the series editor of *Topics in World History*. Romero's articles have appeared in a variety of scholarly journals including the *American Historical Review, Journal of Black Studies, Journal of African Historical Studies, Journal of African History, International Journal of African Historical Studies* and *Cahiers d'Etudes africaines.* Professor Romero has held academic appointments at Johns Hopkins University, and the University of South Florida. She currently teaches history at Towson State University.